Praise for
My Second Chapter

"I remember hearing Second Chapter of Acts for the first time. It captured me on so many levels. But the thing I remember the most was one voice. I had never heard anyone sing like Matthew Ward, whose voice and style are so uniquely his own. His voice was and still is one of the greatest I have ever heard. What a privilege for me to come to know Matthew and learn that the complexities and qualities of his talent don't compare to the compassion of his heart. He has been an example to so many of what it is to walk out one's faith."

—MICHAEL W. SMITH, singer/songwriter and winner
of multiple Grammy Awards

"Matthew Ward believes that since we are all terminal, what's important is what we do with what we've got. Matt has already done a lot with what he got, and I'm glad that one of those things now includes this book. His words ring as bell-clear, just like his one-of-a-kind tenor voice. I found this a charming and disarmingly human read. Not all musicians can write. Matthew Ward has been twice blessed."

—JOHN FISCHER, senior writer of PurposeDrivenLife.com
and author of *Confessions of a Caffeinated Christian*

"As a high-schooler I would try to catch a Second Chapter concert whenever the group was in the area (no up front ticket cost sure helped!). There was always a sense of curiosity about their background, though, as they seemed to shun the contemporary Christian music limelight. Even as I've gotten to know Matthew and his family better, there have always been more unanswered questions—where did Second Chapter's unique sound (and his amazing voice) come from? How did he cope with losing his parents so early in life? What was the early Jesus music scene like? How did his bout with cancer affect him?

Finally Matt answers these questions for each of us who have been so influenced by his music and testimony. From his first days in the Jesus music scene to his continuing solo career, from goofball pranks to a life-and-death bout with cancer, and from early struggles with Christianity to his challenging outlook on today's Christian music, fans like myself finally have the story we've waited for!"

—KURT HEINECKE, Big Idea Inc. director of music, VeggieTales
producer/composer, and six-time winner of the Dove Award

"Reading this book was like getting a backstage pass to watch Matt's life unfold and to see how, from behind the scenes, God shaped both his life and music. Matthew's storytelling made me laugh, cry, and ponder my own journey. How worthwhile to get a close look at the life of the man God uses."

—KEVIN HARRISON, board member of Children's HopeChest
and Chick-fil-A owner/operator

"Funny, sad, moving, inspiring, and sometimes outrageous, *My Second Chapter* is pure undiluted Matthew Ward. Reading this book is just like hearing his story straight from his own mouth: conversational and passionate with not only a clear view into his life and heart but also an inside view into Christian music history (a history he helped create with many others he discusses) and an intimate look inside Second Chapter Acts."

—DEVLIN DONALDSON, cofounder of The Elevation Group
and coauthor of *Pinocchio Nation*

"*My Second Chapter* chronicles the life of one of Christian music's pioneer voices. Both profound and humorous, Matthew takes you on a behind-the-scenes virtual tour of contemporary Christian music's roots as he tells his miraculous story."

—PAUL BALOCHE, recording artist and songwriter
of "Open the Eyes of My Heart"

My 2nd Chapter

Foreword by Darlene Zschech,
writer of one of the world's most celebrated worship songs, "Shout to the Lord"

The Matthew Ward Story

WATERBROOK
PRESS

My Second Chapter
Published by WaterBrook Press
12265 Oracle Boulevard, Suite 200
Colorado Springs, Colorado 80921
A division of Random House Inc.

All Scripture quotations, unless otherwise indicated, are taken from the Holy Bible, New International Version®. NIV®. Copyright © 1973, 1978, 1984 by International Bible Society. Used by permission of Zondervan Publishing House. All rights reserved.

"Easter Song," copyright © 1974, lyrics used by permission of EMI Records, all rights reserved.

The story of the author's childhood appears in a slightly different version in "The Frame Never Outdid the Picture" by Matthew Ward, copyright © 2000–2005 2nd Chapter of Acts, at www.2ndchapterofacts.com/articles/frame-picture.htm.

ISBN 978-1-4000-7080-0

Library of Congress Cataloging-in-Publication Data
Ward, Matthew, 1958–
    My second chapter : the Matthew Ward story / Matthew Ward. — 1st ed.
       p. cm.
    Includes bibliographical references and discography.
    ISBN 978-1-4000-7080-0
    1. Ward, Matthew, 1958– 2. 2nd Chapter of Acts (Musical group) 3. Contemporary Christian music—History and criticism. I. Title.
    ML410.W294A3 2006
    782.25092—dc22
    [B]

                                        2006013901

2006—First Edition

For my wife, Deanne.
Without you, I wouldn't have a second chapter.

And for our daughters, Megin, Morgan, and Mattie,
who have shared their dad with countless people
they will probably never know and whose understanding
of what I do has allowed me the freedom to pursue the race.

Contents

Foreword

When I became a Christian at fifteen years of age, there wasn't a whole lot of contemporary Christian music around—and as a hungry young musician, desperate to serve the Lord with what was in my hand, I began my search for lives to follow.

It was about this time that I received my first Second Chapter of Acts recording—and what an answer to my heart's cry! A single album contained songs that not only lifted me but also taught me the value of a life surrendered to Christ, harmonies that to this day are the finest you'll ever hear, and a voice I could not believe—the voice of Matthew Ward (Mr. Elastic Voice, as he was affectionately known to my friends and me).

I listened, copied, and tried desperately to sing his licks to no avail, and I worshiped the Lord with Matthew and the girls, continuously thanking God for putting the music and hearts of these great ministers into my hands. In fact, for the first couple of years of my Christian walk, I didn't listen to a lot of other music so intensely. (Okay, apart from Matthew's contemporary, Keith Green.)

Years later, as a young married woman involved in her local church music team and leading a vocal department, I worked hard at trying to get similar blends in our harmonies as I'd heard on Second Chapter's incredible records. In fact, on our first few Hillsong Church live worship recordings, Second Chapter's music was the example I used to mirror as our team listened with our ears and hearts to simply exemplary vocals.

I pray that the story of Matthew's journey so far will inspire you, encourage you, and truly present to you the power of a yielded life—not just a talented life. His story has meant everything to me; Matthew, what can I say but thank you?

Thank you for standing, for staying strong, and—without knowing it—for using your gift to minister to a young woman in Australia, mentoring me from afar, setting the bar high for so many like me to aim for.

With much love and respect,

Darlene Zschech, worship pastor at Hillsong Church in Sydney, Australia, author of *Kiss of Heaven,* and writer of "Shout to the Lord"

Preface

Writing a definitive autobiography in seventy thousand words or less is impossible, unless perhaps you've only lived eight or nine years. In this book I've taken a kind of shotgun approach, fitting in the subjects and ideas I felt shaped my life up to this point. For instance, I could write a book on all the places I've been while writing this book—and it would be an adventure, as this story took shape aboard airplanes, ships, on the backs of camels in a Bedouin camp, and while riding elephants through the forests of Thailand, not to mention in countless airports and hotel rooms both in the United States and overseas.

But my purpose in writing this book isn't to impress you with my life. I'm aiming to provide a small window into what it looks like when God shows Himself faithful. The stories I share are meant to expose God, who is not always as serious as people make Him out to be and, on the other hand, who should be feared. God hardly ever does a thing the way I think He will, and His ways are rarely my ways. And that's a real adventure story…

So why do so many Christians I know view God through limited lenses? Why do so many folks either live their lives by some fluid rule of sloppy agape, where grace is cheap and forgiveness comes easy, or by a rigid set of dos and don'ts, where forgiveness is considered a last resort? When God is viewed through either one of these dogmas, fully knowing Him becomes impossible. I've learned there is a balance, and my story is at best a feeble attempt to reveal certain aspects of His character.

A. W. Tozer wrote a book that helped me with some of these questions. In *The Knowledge of the Holy: The Attributes of God,* Tozer makes a good attempt at expressing the idea that all of God's character traits, like Himself, are without limits. In other words, God's grace, love, forgiveness, and understanding know no end. At the same time, His judgment, wrath, and indignation are also boundless.

This view, over the years, has given me a relatively healthy respect for God—allowed me to both love and fear Him. And that's the message I hope my life is. I also hope, then, that this book will inspire you, make you laugh, and at times maybe even make you cry.

My story isn't just about a life, but living it.

1

Second Chapter

The whole house shook from the loud *thump, thump, thump* sounds that jerked me out of a heavy sleep. *What in the world is going on downstairs?* I wondered.

Then I heard a guitar and a man's voice bellow, "I don't know what you came to do, but I just came to praise the Lord!" *Thump, thump, thump.*

I put my head under the pillow, but there was no way I was going to get back to sleep. I got up, pulled on some jeans, and sneaked out onto the landing, where I bumped into my sister Nellie.

It was after 9:00 p.m. and Buck and Annie had sent us off to bed. Both of us were in junior high and had to be up early. My sister and her husband always wanted us to pray with them before we had breakfast and left for school.

I looked at Nellie and shrugged my shoulders. Neither of us knew what was happening, but actually this kind of thing wasn't unusual. People were always coming and going at all hours, friends and strangers stopping by for prayer or to talk about Jesus. We had all recently become born-again Christians, but this lifestyle was pretty strange to me.

Nellie and I edged down the stairway to where we could get a better look. *Wow.*

Immediately I connected the booming voice with his face. When the song ended, Buck spotted both of us. "Hey, you guys, I suppose you can't sleep? Come over here and say hi to Barry McGuire."

Barry McGuire!

Barry was the rock singer who had once been with the New Christy Minstrels before becoming a solo star. One of his monster hits was an anti-war song called "The Eve of Destruction." I knew he had become a born-again Christian too and was now singing the new Jesus music.

Nellie and I said hello to Barry, and then he sang another song or two. He played a twelve-string guitar and sang loudly, using his right foot as his own drum set to stomp out the beat. Thump, thump, thump.

My brother-in-law Buck was a former DJ in AM radio and now was working as a recording engineer at studios in the Los Angeles area. I learned that the two men had met a while back and were thinking about teaming up to record Barry's Christian album.

Having Barry McGuire in our living room was exciting, but it was getting late. About the time it looked like I could head back to bed, Buck freaked me out by saying to Barry, "Do you want to hear my family sing?"

Oh no...not that! I thought. My sisters and I had been doing some singing around the old piano after Nellie and I got home from school. Some friends had heard us and liked what they heard. That had a led to a few gigs at churches, but singing in front of a musician of the caliber of Barry McGuire was something else entirely.

While Buck seemed confident about how Barry would respond, the expression on Barry's face made me think he wasn't so sure! I mean, how many times had Barry McGuire been asked to listen to some amateurs sing a song? What was he going to say, though? "No, I really don't want to hear your family sing"?

There was no time for that. Annie plunged in on her scuffed-up piano, playing a few chords to warm up, then launched into the introduction. Nellie and I joined in on the first verse of one of the tunes Annie had written while we were away at school:

"Hear the bells ringing,
they're singing
that we can be born again.
Hear the bells ringing,
they're singing
Christ is risen from the dead."

As we sang, the look on Barry's face changed.

"The angel up on the tombstone
said, 'He is risen just as He said.
Quickly now, go tell His disciples
that Jesus Christ is no longer dead.'"

A smile began to replace Barry's skeptical look. It seemed he liked what he heard. He even started tapping his foot...

"Joy to the world!
He is risen, hallelujah!
He's risen, hallelujah!
He's risen, hallelujah, hallelujah!"

The song ended, and as the sound of our voices faded, Barry laughed and clapped his hands. We sang another song, and then Nellie and I went back to bed.

Soon thereafter Barry asked Buck to help record his first Jesus music album, *Seeds* (Myrrh 1973). Part of Buck's responsibility was to find backup singers, and he didn't look beyond the dinner table at home. After Barry laid down his vocals, Buck brought Annie, Nellie, and me into the studio, and we recorded the tracks for the background parts.

Later we would tour with Barry, giving us an instant audience and making us more widely known sooner than if we had been on our own. We owe Barry a great debt. He forever changed the way we saw ourselves and the way we would do what we felt the Lord was calling us to.

But our recording of background vocals on Barry's *Seeds* album was actually not the first time I had the experience of recording in a studio.

Jesus Is the Sweetest Name I Know

As my thirteenth birthday approached, Buck, Annie, Nellie, and I had decided to try our hand at recording. Because Buck was in the business, he knew a number of studio musicians in LA. We didn't have the money to hire these experienced guys, but when the studio players got wind of our wishes, they volunteered to play our session for little to nothing. Many of them were the best around.

At the time, we had several friends (some were living with us) we just assumed would be part of our group. One of them was Ed Overstreet. He had written a song called "Jesus Is," and we all decided that should be our first recording. At this time we were in the embryonic stage of what was to become the group. Not only did we not know who would participate, but we hadn't even named the group yet. So after we charted out the song, lined up the musicians, and had them record the instrumental track, everyone assumed Eddie would sing the lead vocal.

As it turned out, the song was in a bad key for him, so Eddie was unable to do the solo. We were sitting around scratching our heads, trying to figure out what to do with the lead vocal, when someone said, "Hey, why don't we let Matt take a shot at it?"

My first thoughts were something like *Um...no, please...not me. Why on earth would you want me to sing that song? I don't know the first thing about singing in a studio. Ahhhhh.*

But the others didn't share my qualms. I was elected.

The recording was scheduled for the day before my thirteenth birthday, in February 1971, at the Mark IV studio in Los Angeles, previously owned by Decca Records. As I walked into studio A, Buck mentioned that it was the same room where Bing Crosby recorded "White Christmas." Strangely, the thought of recording in the same room where the great Bing Crosby cut his tracks wasn't intimidating but instead was somehow comforting. My mom had always been a big fan of Bing's, and maybe the memories of hearing his LP records playing in our home gave me some subconscious comfort.

I've never suffered from a lack of imagination, so while Buck was setting up the microphone, in my mind's eye I caught a glimpse of a studio orchestra playing and Bing crooning away, "I'm dreamin' of a whiiiite Christmas." As the vision of Bing and his band faded, I was left alone in the room with nothing but a set of headphones and a microphone.

Recording with headphones was something that took a little getting used to—it would take about ten years before I felt at home with them. The accompaniment music is piped into your head in a controlled environment, which is very different from singing in "open air." As I listened to the track coming into my ears, Buck made slight adjustments as to how much of my voice I heard in relationship to the instruments and so on.

After I had run through the song a couple of times while Buck made his final tweaks, we started making an earnest effort at recording a good take. By this time my nerves had settled down. When I had finished a run-through of the song, Buck asked me to come into the control room and listen to a replay of my vocal. The tape machine started up, the intro drum fill played right to the down beat, and, as I heard my recorded voice for the first time, I was amazed at how terrible I sounded. As my voice screeched out of the speakers, the sound was completely foreign to what I was used to hearing in my head.

Buck explained to me that for the first time I was hearing my voice outside my own skull, free of the distortion in tones naturally caused by bone conduction. It was a humbling experience, one that I've experienced during every recording project since.

I always tell people I recorded the vocal to "Jesus Is" on my thirteenth birthday. I know I wrote earlier that I went in the studio *the day before* my birthday. Actually, both days are accurate, because after we finished that first vocal, Buck somehow managed to erase what I had just recorded. (I wonder if that ever happened to Bing.) I got to come back to the studio the next day, on my birthday, and do it all over again.

Because the production of an album is expensive, Buck began shopping our sample recorded song to some record labels, seeing if someone would help fund a complete record. He would play "Jesus Is" to the executives, and after they heard the song, invariably they would ask, "Who's the black girl singing that song?" You can imagine that as a thirteen-year-old boy, I was offended at being referred to as a girl. However, I've come to accept the fact that I indeed sounded like one, which should have been no surprise, because I'd grown up listening to all the great Motown groups.

So often in those early days we were shooting in the dark; we had no preconceived notion as to what we should or shouldn't pursue. The idea that we were a "Christian group" did not stop us from going after a secular recording deal. At that time Christian labels were rare, and we knew of none interested in signing a group making the kind of music we believed we were supposed to record. Our primary purpose was to get the gospel to people; we didn't worry about how it got there.

It would be a few years before the Christian music industry would even exist. The term "contemporary Christian music" was still a phrase waiting to be invented (and one that I have never cared much for). In the early days the term "Jesus music" was the accepted idiom. It seems to me that it wasn't until the Christian music industry started watering down the gospel to the point that many times it was impossible to tell Christian from secular music that a new descriptive term was needed.

We Need a Name

We knew we were supposed to be ministering our songs to people, so we began to take on engagements around the LA area. The venues consisted mostly of coffeehouses that were located in the basements of churches or near church properties. For a while we could get away with being known as Annie, Nellie, and Matthew—the "two sisters and little brother group," but the time came when we definitely needed a name.

Buck was probably the most eager to come up with something to call us, because he was pitching the group to record companies. He told us several times, "We need to find a name. Let's talk about it and pray." So we did, but nothing came of it.

One day Buck was at work editing a commercial, and as clear as day, in his mind he heard "Second Chapter of Acts." He quickly wrote it down so he wouldn't forget it. When he came home, he said, "The Lord gave me a name for the group."

We all asked, "What is it?"

"Second Chapter of Acts."

We couldn't believe it! Who would call a singing group *that?* With no disrespect to the Lord, we thought it was a horrible name. It was too long. It didn't sound like two sisters and a brother. It seemed clueless!

Buck let us vent for a few minutes and then said, "Well, why don't we all just go to our rooms and read the second chapter of Acts?" To be honest, I didn't know what was in that chapter. So the girls and I went to our rooms. I opened up my Bible and soon found out that a lot happens in Acts 2. First there's Pentecost, then Peter gives a rocking sermon, after which thousands are saved and baptized. And then follows the story of all the believers being together and experiencing many signs and wonders. The Christians found favor with everyone, and the church grew by leaps and bounds.

Annie, Nellie, and I came back down to the kitchen. We were overwhelmed, nearly speechless. We were all thinking that this New Testament chapter pretty well sums up the story of Jesus and what the church is supposed to be about. Finally Annie said, "I guess if God wants to call us Second Chapter of Acts, that's amazing. It would be an honor."

And it always was an honor—through all seventeen years, the recording, the traveling, the sharing of our music about Jesus, the good times and hard times.

The Lord gave the group a special name. And there's more to the story...

2

Youngest of Nine

My earliest memory is of a woman falling down a flight of stairs, crashing through a screen door, and landing on the porch outside. The stairs, screen door, and porch belonged to the house I lived in as a child. The woman was my mother.

Not long after my birth, my mother was diagnosed with epilepsy. Too bad the diagnosis was incorrect, which was not discovered until years later. Mom actually had a benign brain tumor that affected her balance and caused other problems with her health. If the tumor had been found early and treated properly, she might have lived a long and active life. I'll never know.

What I do recall, in fleeting wisps of memory, is that Mommy was sick. She was the woman who didn't move much, always lying on the sofa or in bed, shuffling to sit in a chair for hours on end, often in the dark, seemingly doing nothing, able only to watch the family chaos swirl around her. She played less and less of a role in our family's life.

I learned from the family historians that the Wards got their start in a blizzard. What else would you expect? It was North Dakota. And did I tell you it was *cold?*

One wintry day at the time school let out, my father, Walter Samuel

Ward, was driving a truck through his hometown of Grand Forks, North Dakota. A young schoolteacher named Kathrine Elizabeth Irmen (she went by Elizabeth) was leading some students through knee-deep snow toward the main road. Walter slid his truck to a stop, threw open the passenger door, and yelled, "Come on, kids! Pile in! I'll get you home."

Pile in they did. Then Walter asked Elizabeth, "And where do you live, honey?" It was an innocent question. Elizabeth was so young that he'd mistaken her for one of the students.

"Well, *honey,*" she replied, "I just live around the corner. I'm the teacher."

Oops. The awkward beginning must have not discouraged anyone. The two young people fell in love and married in the Roman Catholic Church.

Babies started arriving with stunning regularity. The first five, in order, were Stephanie, Irmen, Kathryn (Kathy), Franklin (Frank), and Anne (Annie). After a pause of a few years—I guess even Catholics sometimes take a break—the final foursome arrived: Anthony (Tony), Jack, Nellie, and me. I was born on February 15, 1958.

My mother had quit teaching in order to raise us children. My memories of her are limited, but my older brothers and sisters have told me that she was an intelligent, well-educated, and talented woman. Mom played the piano as Stephanie, Kathy, and Annie sang old favorites like "How Much Is That Doggie in the Window?" They must have sounded decent. Word got out about "The Ward Sisters," who entertained at all sorts of rural festivities: farm co-op meetings, school openings, church picnics.

All that ended before I came along, however, due to my mother's worsening health. Years later I learned that Elizabeth was an accomplished pianist. During her illness, one of the places my mom did not sit was on the piano bench. I never heard her play a note.

My father made music too. He loved to sing and played the harmonica. And he danced in the kitchen. He had a wacky sense of humor, which explains some things about how I view and encounter the world. Earlier in his life Walter had tried different schemes to make money, some of them a bit brave, like running moonshine. By the time I came along, though, my dad's responsibility to feed and clothe his family, which was larger than some towns in North Dakota, meant he worked hard at any job he could find to make ends meet. Most of the time he was a sharecropper, earning a sparse wage from farmers near where we lived in a house bursting with exuberant humanity in the subarctic city of Grand Forks. We were there until I was five.

It's Cold

North Dakota. What can I say? I lived there when I was a little kid growing up in a herd of children where there was an endless supply of creative foolishness, fun, and laughter. Oh, and North Dakota was cold—wear-three-coats-and-never-take-off-your-mittens *cold.*

One winter day, when I was probably four, my brothers and I were playing in a field across the street from our house. The field was blanketed by snow that was both thick and hard enough to allow innovative tunneling. We soon had a marvelous snow fort that we were prepared to defend at any cost.

My brothers, who had done most of the work getting our underground (or "under-snow") world in place, became aware of some neighbor kids who occupied the other end of the field with their own snow fort. My brothers and I—never the kinds of guys to lie down and play dead—soon decided that the newcomers had to be neutralized.

The first order of business was to stockpile ammunition, which meant making as many snowballs as possible in the shortest amount of time. As the battle over turf was about to heat up, we put our strategy together. I would take up the rear, which at first I thought was an honored position, only to realize later that my brothers were trying to get me out of the way and protect me.

As the icy grenades started to fly, I was amazed at how far my brothers could throw those frozen balls of destruction. I, being so young, had only enough strength to fling a snowball a few feet. I couldn't understand why, as the battle ensued, my brothers didn't give me more ammunition.

The Ward gang wasted the opposition, partly I'm sure because I don't think we fought fairly: more than one of our snowballs contained some rocks. What can I say? We were kids.

On another winter day, my brother Tony invented a game involving his Erector set. He and another brother, Jack, hung sections of the set out the second-story window of our house, lowering them to ground level and then cranking them back up. Inevitably, a piece would fall off and disappear in the snowbank below the window.

"Hey, Matt! Go get that piece, will you?" they would say. These guys were my heroes, so eagerly off I would go. I didn't know why they found this so funny, but both of them laughed hysterically as I dug around in the snow for the missing sections of the Erector set. So what if it was twenty degrees below zero and I was wearing nothing more than my birthday suit? I loved making my brothers laugh, so I started rolling buck naked in the freezing snow pile to get the desired response.

Such antics aside, keeping warm was an important priority there on the Dakota tundra. Our family was poor, and coal cost money. So I can recall two times when my dad chose to use—shall we say—alternative fuel sources for our furnace.

On one occasion he stole a telephone pole waiting to be put into service that was lying next to the road. I don't know how he got the thing home; maybe he dragged it behind our truck. Anyway, he chopped the pole into chunks and began feeding them into the furnace. There was only one problem: the pole had been treated with the tar-based substance creosote to keep it from rotting. That wood sure burned black!

Another time, Dad threw a car tire into the furnace. He had quite a time explaining to the fire department why black smoke was pouring out our chimney.

My dad's way of doing things was unique, but I always admired how he would never let his family go without the basics, whether that meant finding food, providing heat, or whatever. The smoke and pollution spewing from our chimney may have smelled up the neighborhood, but one thing I knew for sure: we would never freeze or starve to death.

California, Here We Come

When I was five, on a sunny summer day in 1963, our family went to a barbecue near our home. Suddenly, my mom fell backward out of her seat at the picnic table. I saw her on the ground, foam dripping from her mouth.

Her health was failing fast, so my parents decided to leave North Dakota and move to Sacramento, California, where my mother's sister, my aunt Ruthie Preston, and her family lived. The plan made sense to have Mom near family members who could help take care of her and support the rest of us, and I believe my Uncle Clyde assured my father that he could get a better job in Sacramento than he had in Grand Forks.

So my father loaded our belongings into a truck and drove to California, taking some of the older children with him. (My oldest sister, Stephanie, was already married, and she stayed in North Dakota.) The rest of the Ward clan boarded a train heading west. This was a dramatic experience for me, the most exciting adventure yet in my young life. The trip took several days, and I wished it would last even longer.

My eyes could not take in this new, flowing world fast enough. Up to that point my memories had involved mostly static pictures of the world around me. To go from a rural existence, where my life was composed of short clips and still-frame images, to one that was full of new sights, sounds, and smells running in a continuous stream, was almost overwhelming. I loved it.

Life aboard the train held more wonders and adventures than I thought possible. There were visual treats day after day, as the ever-changing landscape outside the train windows presented us with rivers, mountains, valleys, and plains.

At one point our train crossed an old trestle bridge that spanned a deep river valley. I recall sticking my head out the train window and feeling that there was no earth below us and we were floating on air across a bottomless abyss. This was the first time I felt a fear of heights, afraid I might be sucked out the window and plummet to the bottom below.

My favorite times on the train were mealtimes. Food was served in the dining car, which had two levels. The first level was of little interest to me; it was much the same as the rest of the train, except it had some tables in place of rows of seats. The second level, however, was something else: a ceiling of clear Plexiglas, allowing the most outstanding views the train had to offer. Of all the places to explore aboard, nothing else came close to the bubble car, as we came to call it.

At first the bubble car was just an amazing world of light and sound for me, with trees flying by at eye level, but it soon became my favorite hangout for another reason. Crawling under the tables of this mobile restaurant, I discovered treasures beyond my wildest dreams—pocket change left as tips, which had tumbled to the floor. I had never seen so much money, which I crammed into my pockets. Needless to say, I couldn't wait for mealtimes.

At Home in Sacramento

Upon our arrival in California, we lived for a short time with my aunt and uncle, but eventually we bought a house a few miles away in Rancho Cordova. Our new house was very small—about nine hundred square feet in all—but we had a lot of good times there in spite of its size. Maybe even because of it.

With so many people living under such a small roof, the kids didn't spend much time indoors. The weather in Sacramento was a welcome improvement over Grand Forks; it was nice to be outside so much of the time without layers of clothing. I'm sure no one appreciated the weather more than my mom—it got us out of her hair for most of the day.

As we settled into life in California, my dad looked for work and was employed as a maintenance worker for the airplane manufacturer McDonnell Douglas for a short time. The Wards in general, though, seem to have a hard time working for other people, so it didn't take Dad long to realize that he would have to find a line of work that suited him better—something he could control. He chose to paint houses. This was a job he would stick with until his dying day.

The older boys were enlisted to help in the new family business. Throughout my childhood, I was lucky enough not to have to do all the really hard things my brothers did. In North Dakota I never had to do farm chores since our family moved to a house in town just before I was born. In Sacramento I was too young to help with the painting, but many times I watched my dad and brothers, after a hard day of painting, clean out their paintbrushes and sprayer heads.

I liked being around my dad and had a habit of staying up late with him, watching the news or whatever else came on so that I wouldn't have to go to bed (always the night owl). On one of these nights I was introduced to the most amazing music I'd ever heard. The year was 1964—I was just six years old. The program was *The Ed Sullivan Show*, and there on the tube, playing live for the first time in the United States, was a band called The Beatles. It was hard to hear them over the screaming of the studio audience, but I heard enough that night to know that music would forever hold a special place in my life.

Meanwhile, I spent my days exploring a new fascination that flowed just three blocks from our new house. The American River begins in the Sierra Nevada mountains, runs through California's capital city of Sacramento, and then joins the Sacramento River before emptying into San Francisco Bay. The American River is where gold was discovered at Sutter's Mill, leading to the California gold rush of 1849.

What an awesome playground the river became—an endless source of adventure! I couldn't wait to see what lay beyond the next bend. There were rapids one moment and calm, open waters the next. We soon had two places we frequented the most, "the clay cliffs" and "sandy beach."

The clay cliffs were closer to our house. They stretched along the riverfront for several hundred yards and consisted of ledges and outcroppings that varied in height up to thirty feet or more. Before long we were jumping off the highest of these points into the river below, which was a challenge because unless you ran as fast as you could (and I mean as *fast* as you could) before you jumped, you would hit earth and not water.

Near the clay cliffs is where I learned to swim. I never was much of a surface swimmer. To me the joy of swimming came from holding my breath and swimming as long as I possibly could underwater. I guess the future singer was already building up his lung capacity. I was surprisingly swift underwater, many times beating those swimming on top of the water.

Growing up with this giant baby-sitter was one of life's greatest joys. The river never complained, smarted off, or made fun of you. However, the river demanded respect or it might kill you.

We had a name for the part of the river people didn't respect enough— dead man's bend. It had claimed enough lives to warrant the name. One time I was shooting the rapids just ahead of dead man's bend when I was overcome by panic and nearly drowned. A man on shore saw me flailing around and swam out to save me. Without his bravery, I would have been a goner.

Target Practice

One time, when we were playing along the American River, my oldest brother, Irmen, brought his automatic rifle with him for a little target practice. (He had somehow smuggled the rifle home following his stint in the military.) Irmen shot up just about every available target, such as a milk carton we found, with a steady stream of bullets while the rest of us stood nearby, watching in amazement.

As silence fell after the last burst of shells, Irmen thought he had switched on the safety. He had not. I was standing next to him, with my hand inches from the muzzle, when Irmen started playing with the trigger and bullets poured out the end of the barrel. Luckily for me, I wasn't standing any closer than I was, or I would have lost one of my feet—or at least a mess of toes.

The sandy beach was further away. We had to walk a mile or two from our house down a gravel road to get there. I remember the smells along the way, the strongest coming from the anise plants beside the roadway. The setting of the beach was spectacular, like a scene in a movie. The beach, which was about four hundred yards long, started at the top of a hill and sloped to the river below. Here we swam and messed around for countless hours.

Fishing for Food

Salmon in large numbers ran the American River, and one year my brothers had an idea for catching some of these slippery brutes. Their fishing method involved attaching fishing line to an arrow and using a bow to shoot a salmon as it passed by. When a fish was successfully harpooned, we simply pulled in the line.

This fishing technique was wildly successful, and soon we were each holding one or more salmon on the bank. Then we heard yelling from downstream. To our surprise, a game warden had been watching us with his binoculars. Needless to say, what we were doing was incredibly illegal.

The game warden headed our way, so we took to the woods. What an adrenaline rush! Our escape was complicated by the flopping fish, but there was no way we were going to let go of them. Not only had we gone to a lot of work to catch them, but our family needed the food. So we ran over stumps and rocks and slid down hills, our arms full of squirming salmon. We stayed ahead of the game warden because we knew that part of the river valley far better than he did. But he was gaining on us.

"We can't outrun this guy carrying these fish," Tony said, as we halted behind some bushes. The arrows were still tucked in the salmon, making transporting them a challenge. "You know those holes away from the riverbank that have water in them? Let's store the fish there."

So that's what we did, leaving just enough of the arrows (which were still sticking in the fish) protruding above the surface of the water so we could see the tops of the feathers later.

With the sounds of the game warden on our trail still echoing in the woods, we hightailed it home.

After we cooled our heals at home for a while, one of the older boys said to Dad, "We, um…caught some, uh…fish down at the river."

"Well, where are they?" he asked.

We told him the whole story. We held our breath, not knowing how Dad would react to our brilliant yet law-breaking approach to fishing. As it turned out, he armed us with flashlights and said something like, "Don't get caught. Bring home the meat."

As we tried to locate the fish in the dark, we kept looking over our shoulders, but the game warden was nowhere to be seen. It didn't occur to us that the warden had quit the chase long ago and was sitting at home watching television. The idea of leaving the arrow feathers just out of the water paid off, since we could easily see them as we flashed our lights across the puddles. To our surprise, all the fish were still breathing when we pulled them up.

I didn't care much for fish back then, but the rest of the Wards dined on fine salmon for a week or more.

Dreamer

My family being Roman Catholic, we attended Mass regularly at St. John Vianney Church in Rancho Cordova, and I was enrolled at the school attached to the church. Although I hated the nuns who served as both teachers and disciplinarians at my school (one beat the tar out of me in class one day), and although I understood little that went on in our church services, I still believed strongly in the existence of God, and thoughts of Him filled me with wonder. That spiritual sensitivity came out in a surprising way one day when I was seven or eight years old.

My dad had built an extra bedroom for Jack and me in the garage. One summer morning, when my dad and brothers were off painting a house somewhere, I was lying on my bed, daydreaming. Suddenly, I felt an uncontrollable urge to draw a picture on the wall over my bed. I grabbed a pencil and, kneeling there on my bed, started to draw. It felt as though I wasn't the one drawing; it felt more like I was watching someone else drawing with my hand. Although at first I didn't know what my hand was drawing, what took shape looked like a church. I could see into the building and discern there what appeared to be an altar.

After my hand had put the final touches on this work of art, I went to get my mom so she could take a look at the results of my hand's possession. She took one look at the drawing, and I could tell by her expression that she was genuinely impressed with her youngest son's handiwork. Instead of getting mad that I had drawn on the wall, she praised my work and let it go at that. (A few days later my dad painted over my work; I guess he wasn't as much of an art lover as Mom.)

I won't try to interpret where this drawing came from or exactly what it meant to me then or later. But I can tell you that being used to draw that church was a combined spiritual and artistic experience that moved my young heart and deposited a memory in my mind that I will never forget.

Along with my drawing on the wall, one other experience from that period in my life seems, as I look back, to show how God was even then reaching out to me and beginning to awaken the creativity He had placed within me.

Many nights I would dream that I was riding a horse as fast as I could, being chased by a group of people (Indians, I think). I would ride my horse to the edge of a tall cliff and, realizing I had no other way to escape my pursuers, keep riding the horse at full speed until we passed right over the cliff. My horse and I would plummet for what seemed a very long time. Just before I would hit the bottom, I would wake up, sitting bolt upright in my bed, with the feeling that I had almost become one with the ground.

To that point, my recurring dream was nothing special. But then one night I had an extension of the dream that would never be repeated, much as I have wished it would. Again the riding pell-mell toward the cliff. Again the fall toward the ground. This time, though, instead of waking up before I hit the bottom, I felt myself smashing straight into the ground. What happened next has left an impression in my mind that I can neither account for nor forget.

After auguring into the ground, I had the distinct sensation of floating up out of my mangled body. When I looked momentarily down at my lifeless hulk, I was soon whisked away to a different scene. I was in a new world that I can hardly describe, but at the time it seemed more real than any other place I had ever been. (This new world did not amaze me just because I was a little kid; I know that if I saw those things again today, I would be just as amazed.)

I began to hear sounds like I'd never heard before. And with these sounds came translucent, colored shapes floating in the air. I soon realized that the sounds were emanating from these shapes. Each color shape had a different sound.

Every once in a while, these colorful sound-shapes collided with one another. The interesting thing was that as the collisions took place, instead of bouncing off one another, the shapes passed through one another. As they momentarily blended together, they took on one another's color and sound characteristics, creating for a few seconds completely new sounds and colors. And after they passed through one another, they returned to their original conditions.

To this day, I have no idea what I was hearing and seeing, and I don't really care. Was this heaven? Was it a foreshadowing of the way I would later ornament a melody in singing praise to God? I don't know. But I do know that this unique dream made me more aware of spiritual realms and caused me to think more about God and eternity.

Sunrise

When I was ten, in the summer of 1968, my mother's physical condition became much worse. For years, she had been weakening and had occasionally suffered seizures, leading to the diagnosis of epilepsy. But now she began losing her balance regularly and lost control of her bodily functions. My dad took her to the hospital, where the doctors ran a series of tests on her.

The brain tumor that the doctors found, while benign, was the size of a grown man's fist and was interfering with her brain function. The doctors performed surgery on her, but it was too late. She lived through the surgery but died shortly afterward because the trauma was more than her system could handle.

Following her operation, I went to visit my mother for the last time early in the morning, while it was still dark. Mom was conscious, and she told my brother Irmen, "I just want to see the sunrise. I know that if I see the sunrise, I will be all right."

She didn't see the sunrise.

At least not in this world.

Through the death of my mother and the funeral that followed, I never felt angry toward God. In fact, I had an odd peace about the situation. That's not to say I didn't have my share of questions, but I knew we all had our time to go, and who was I to question the timing? Where this fledgling trust in God came from, I cannot say.

On the day my mother was buried, we were all sitting around in our home and talking when suddenly my father made a bizarre statement. In the presence of all us children, he announced that he would be dead in two years. We all thought he was nuts, because at this point my father was as healthy and as strong as a horse.

Now, here's the weirdest deal: my father died two years to the day after my mother was buried.

3

Running Wild

Many mornings after my mother died, I would get up to have breakfast before school and find my father sitting in a chair beside the kitchen table, incredibly still, staring off into space. In one hand he held a coffee cup, and in the other a cigarette, often ignored until the lengthening ash came perilously close to dropping off. The smoke formed a thin column that stretched in a straight line toward the ceiling.

I've never since observed a more perfect stillness nor heard a louder silence.

We could tell Dad missed Mom terribly, but he kept up a strong front for his kids. Always a hard worker, Dad worked even more throughout this difficult time. I imagine this was his way of keeping his mind off the loss of his love. During the last two years of my dad's life, the spark that had driven him was gone, and much of his life was just punching the clock and going through the motions.

In this state, Dad was unable to cope well by himself with the four of us children who were still living at home, most of us teenagers by this point. This inability perhaps affected me, as the youngest, more than the others. Although I'd been getting too little discipline and guidance already, I got even less after my mother died.

Even when Mom was alive, by the time I'd joined the Ward clan, most of the rules that had applied to my older siblings didn't carry much weight anymore. Mom, who normally would have doled out the discipline, was too sick to bother. Dad had been so busy just keeping the household running that he didn't step in to discipline me unless I'd done something that made him mad.

Like the time I put rocks in the clothes dryer so when my mom put in a load of clothes the dryer sounded like a giant rock polisher. Dad whacked me for that.

The only other time Dad gave me some well-deserved painful love and hit me was the night my brother Jack and I mocked him. Dad had a nervous habit of bobbing his head, like he was perpetually nodding a yes to an invisible visitor. This bobbing was the worst when he watched television. One night Jack and I were mimicking Dad's head movement, bob for bob, and not realizing Dad had stopped viewing television and was watching us instead. Out of the blue my dad slapped me across the face so hard I saw stars. After that, if I decided to do any mimicking, I made sure I wasn't the one sitting within his reach.

Dad did the best he could after Mom died, but his own intimate world had shattered, and he didn't have the energy to help all of us work through our loss. I know now, after living as much life as I have, that negative psychological seeds were planted in my mind during the two-year span between the deaths of my mother and father. I began developing a protective shell that hardened over time, a shell that would keep people, especially women, at arm's length. I didn't want to hurt again the way I did after Mom went away. I had lost the center of my universe and didn't have much of a moral compass. Yes, my mom was ill from my earliest memories, but she still had a way of speaking into my heart like only a mother can. She always retained the ability to act as anchor and center of my moral world, despite her weaknesses.

I had people around me, including a small group of friends at parochial school. But I was fending for myself when it came to issues of the heart. In some ways, I began to live more like an animal than a human.

One thing kept me from getting into more trouble—my belief in the Golden Rule: "Do to others what you would have them do to you." My brothers instilled that rule in me. They lived by it themselves (more or less). The rule helped, but I became a wild kid.

Many times in the summer, especially after Mom's death, I hung around outside with Dad, my brothers, and the next-door neighbors. They would

Radio

While we were living in Rancho Cordova, my dad converted all but a few feet of our garage into an extra bedroom. (The remaining few feet he walled off and kept as a place in which to stow his painting supplies.) This extra bedroom had no windows and would stay dark even after the arrival of the sun.

We had an old AM radio in that bedroom. The radio used vacuum tubes that emitted light, which would stream through small holes in the backing of the radio and splash in various shapes against the wall. I would stare at the light for hours while listening to music. I believe that the sounds (mostly Motown stuff) coming from that radio in that room shaped my love for music more than any other single thing.

all stand around our yard drinking beer, from time to time setting their cans on top of the fence posts. When one of the guys got wrapped up and distracted in telling a story—wham!—I'd grab the beer and slam it back. I was crafty. Just before they'd notice what I was doing, I'd set the beer back on the post. I hardly ever got caught.

I came to enjoy the alcohol buzz and grabbed a quick drink anytime I could.

Once I went to a wedding reception at my Aunt Ruthie's house, where everyone was drinking champagne. The glasses had long, fluted stems that held a little champagne after a person had finished the drink. I ran around the house, looking for abandoned goblets. I found plenty. Some of the ones I snagged had more than a little champagne left, and after a while I was quite tipsy. No telling how much champagne I drank that day.

Around the same time, I met Jerry, one of my brothers' friends. Jerry fascinated me because he was missing part of a finger. I finally got up the courage to ask him, "How did you lose your finger?"

"I was cutting off a rattlesnake's head," he claimed, "but I wasn't careful enough, because the head of the snake still bit me somehow."

Okay.

Besides his missing finger, Jerry had other problems—like drinking. He liked cheap red wine that came in gallon-size glass jugs. On a fine summer afternoon, Jerry would find a comfortable spot up the hill from the river and start sipping. By the time his jug was half empty, the wine, the dry warm air, and the shade of the trees had taken their toll. He was out like a light.

As soon as Jerry dozed off, I would lift his jug and sneak off to some secluded area where I finished off the wine while watching the river roll lazily by. Jerry never said anything to me about the missing wine—he may not have known how much of the jug he drank.

Jerry was around just one summer; after that we lost contact with him. Years later I heard that he was dead, killed when a train ran over him. I suppose alcohol had something to do with that.

Did I drink to blunt the pain I felt after losing Mom? I have no idea. It did make me feel good, that I know. But starting to swear after Mom died—I don't think that had much to do with my grief. I just got a kick out of shocking people. And I suppose it made me feel grown-up or tough or something.

It got to the point where just about every other word out of my mouth was an obscenity. At first I loved the look on people's faces when they would see this sweet-looking child swearing like a sailor. But then my dirty talk began to cause problems.

My mouth became so bad that my brothers wouldn't hang out with me. That hurt, so I began cleaning up my tongue. I was surprised by how hard it was to stop swearing. It had become such a natural way of speaking for me that it took the better part of three years to completely rid myself of the habit.

Pyromania

I loved to watch things burn. I especially liked torching those little green plastic army men, which were cheap and came by the hundreds in clear plastic bags.

My brother Jack and I had discovered a way to climb through the rafters above the garage into an area that remained open above the washer and dryer. We found that a couple of boards placed in the V-shaped supports of the rafters made a perfect chair. Sitting in our "chair," we gathered our army troops and held burning matches to their heads. As the plastic melted and began to drip, each drop made the most amazing sound—a kind of a *zzzziiiiiiiiipp*—before it hit the concrete floor below.

It wasn't long before I was burning all kinds of plastic toys. The main difference was that I started doing most of my burning outdoors. I can recall two times when I caught more than toys on fire. (I was really good at starting fires, but not so good at making sure they were out.)

One day, shortly after getting home from one of my burning episodes, I heard the sound of approaching sirens. Curious, I went outside to find out what the commotion was about. I saw that several fire trucks had arrived at the location of my latest burning. Apparently, the brush near where I'd been melting plastic toys had ignited, and now the fire was out of control and consuming a field. Several houses nearby were in jeopardy. Firefighters were scrambling around the trucks, pulling out hoses, getting everything prepared to battle the blaze.

As I watched the fire I had started turning into a disaster, I came face to face with an angry homeowner. The man picked me up off the ground, stared me straight in the eye, and yelled, "Did you have anything to do with that fire?"

Now, I ask you, what would you have said? Keeping as straight and innocent a face as I could, I looked him right back in the eye and began lying like a banshee. "I had nothing to do with the fire," I said, my voice shaking.

He didn't seem convinced.

"No sir," I continued. "It wasn't me, sir." (I think that was the first time in my life I ever used the term "sir.")

After he grilled me for a few more moments, getting nothing out of me other than my "No sir" comments, he set me back down.

I hung around just long enough to appear innocent before hightailing it back home. Luckily, the fire was put out before it did any real property damage.

I did start one other fire that summer, causing a bit more property damage. My pyro adventures stopped after that. I guess the thought of doing damage to somebody else's stuff outweighed the fun of melting toys.

My Bicycle

No one in my family had a bicycle. That was an unaffordable luxury, so we walked everywhere. In the heat of summer, walking along the gravel road that paralleled the American River, watching all my friends riding their bicycles, I craved a bike.

One day a friend of mine, Don Guy, showed up at my front door with the strangest excuse for a bike I'd ever seen. Don told me that he had found it, though I learned later it was stolen. Don had stripped it down to the frame, then reassembled it with all kinds of weird parts. The frame and a few other items were British, while all the other parts were American—not a happy marriage. Nothing worked really right on that bike, but I rode it everywhere.

One day I got ahold of an old barbecue grill and with a screwdriver removed two of the legs. It looked like I could take a hammer and tap those grill legs directly over the forks on my bike, giving my already strange-looking contraption an extended front end. I thought that would look really groovy, like the motorcycles my older brothers rode.

The bike became more freakish by the day. Not only did it have a huge front end, but the only tire I could find for the front was from a bike twice its size. As I rode down the block, I learned to pop wheelies. The only problem was that with the oversized tire in the front and the tiny one in back, no one knew I was doing wheelies because the front tire only lifted about an inch before the bike would flip over backward.

I loved the new freedom my bike gave me and rode all hours of the day and night. I quickly learned that it was more comfortable to ride during the cooler hours of the evening. I never had to check in or get permission before taking off on my excursions. Since no one seemed to miss me much, many times I stayed out until one or two in the morning before finding my way home.

On many of these evenings, I rounded up a few riding buddies. With a pack of us riding shoulder to shoulder down the street, we would distract the kid riding closest to the curb. Before he knew what was going on, we guided him smack-dab into the back end of a parked car. As his bike came to a sudden stop, he would fly over its handlebars, landing on the car's trunk. More than a few fights broke out after we all had a laugh at someone else's expense.

I got duped only once. Out of the corner of my eye, I saw that I was closing fast on the rear end of a car, but at the last moment I was able to jam my brakes and didn't collide. I stopped playing that trick on people after that.

Vintage Ward

One day while my brothers and I were floating down the river in the area just past dead man's bend, we noticed a bunch of grapes growing wild at the water's edge. Irmen decided the grapes could be used for wine. He concocted a plan that involved using his huge rubber raft—the kind you see at raft rental places—and recruiting his younger siblings to pick grapes, with a promise that if we helped, our wages would be a considerable amount of the finished product. Since I had already developed a taste for wine, I was excited about the possibilities.

The day came for Irmen to put his plan into motion, and we all piled into the car. Obviously, there was no room for the raft, so we stuck our arms out the windows and held the raft secure on the roof. We hauled the raft to the river, then after jockeying for prime seating spots, floated to the grape site.

A finger of water running away from the river led into the heart of the grapevines. We realized that it was infinitely easier to pick the grapes in this protected area than by the side of the river where the swift current threatened to take the raft downstream every few seconds. But there were downsides to picking away from the river. First, the vegetation was so thick, and there was no breeze, which made it unbearably hot. Second, the horseflies were on the warpath.

At this point the Ward mentality kicked into high gear, which meant we all picked grapes furiously. We loved the idea of free grapes, but we weren't going to give the horseflies any more flesh than necessary.

Soon the raft brimmed with grapes. Our attention shifted to the new task at hand—getting this precious cargo back to the car. We were fortunate from the standpoint that, though the current was swift, the water was relatively shallow. Slipping and sliding, we ferried the grape-laden raft to the other side of the river.

After landing on the far shore, we realized it would be nearly impossible to carry the grape-filled raft all the way to the car. So we all helped to pull the raft upstream along the shore until we were near the area where we had parked the car. From there, it was just grunt work. (I have no idea what the raft weighed, but it was a lot. If you picture a four- to six-man raft filled to overflowing with grapes, you'll get an idea.) We finally reached the car and somehow hoisted the raft up onto the roof. None of us had to worry about holding the raft down this time—it wasn't going anywhere.

After arriving home, we pulled the raft off the car roof and muscled it around to the backyard. There we dumped the grapes into a large plastic kiddy pool. After we had hosed off our feet, we jumped into the pool and began mashing the grapes with our feet. It reminded me of an *I Love Lucy* episode, as one by one we slipped and fell, then got back up, laughing hysterically, covered from head to toe with grape juice.

Once the fun was over, with all of us sticky and hot and with every grape smashed to pulp, we took the extracted liquid out of the pool and transferred it to a large ceramic crock. My brother Irmen took the crock around to the garage, where it was cool and dark. He did certain things to the juice (added sugar and whatever else) to cause it to ferment. Then we just had to wait.

In the weeks that followed, Irmen checked on his concoction from time to time. To me, it seemed like an eternity. I think a problem with his plan, at least the fermenting part, was that he never sealed the crock properly. On more than one occasion, I checked on the wine myself and noticed a lot of fruit flies or gnats hovering over it and even getting into the crock.

After the allotted time for fermentation had passed, we went to the garage to taste our new batch of wine. Our hearts instantly sank. Instead of enjoying the most wonderful wine in the world, which we really thought it would be, we tasted the most tart, labor-intensive batch of vinegar ever made.

After this escapade, I became reluctant to jump into just any harebrained idea my brothers conjured up.

The Impossible Again

I can't point to one particular day when I knew my dad was ill. I was just a kid, so I wasn't aware of everything that was going on. And besides, even if I'd had an inkling, I wasn't willing to entertain the thought of my dad being seriously sick. The death of my mom was still fresh in my mind. All my friends still had their mothers, so to me her passing was more of a fluke than anything. It was just unimaginable that my father might die as well.

My dad started not feeling well. He went to see a doctor, and not long after that, I heard the word leukemia for the first time. One day, after a hospital visit, my dad walked into the house and his legs looked twice their normal size. One of my older brothers pulled me aside and told me that Dad's legs were swollen because of the blood transfusions they were giving him.

I had a hard time grasping how ill he really was. I couldn't think of a time when I'd seen my dad sick; he was always so strong and healthy. He failed quickly. Watching his body break down was hard for me to understand. I kept hoping his strength would return, but he seemed to get worse by the day.

One morning, as I was passing his room, I saw him sitting on the edge of his bed. He had one shoe on and was struggling with the other. I started to walk on, but he called my name. As I approached him, he said to me in a raspy whisper, "Help me...tie my...shoes."

As I began tightening the laces, I heard his labored breathing, coming in short shallow gasps. I knew something was terribly wrong. Later I found out that his lungs were full of fluid. He was literally drowning in his own blood.

I was so frightened that I didn't know what to do. I think he saw the terror in my eyes, and with short phrases he told me someone was coming to take him to the hospital. That morning, I watched others help him to the car and drive away. He left without even a wave. It was the last time I saw my dad alive.

Nothing was ever the same again.

4

At Home with Buck and Annie

My world had turned upside down and inside out. Both my mother and father were gone. For starters, where would I live?

In the summer of 1970, four of us—Tony, Jack, Nellie, and I—were still living in our little house in Sacramento. I would have liked to stay there, near the enticing waters of the American River, but wiser heads in the family decided that Nellie and I, who were the youngest at fourteen and twelve, needed to go someplace where grownups would look out for us. Tony and Jack went to live with our older brother Irmen and his wife, Betty.

I was given two options: I could move in with our Aunt Ruthie and Uncle Clyde Preston in Sacramento, who had children of their own, or I could go to Los Angeles and live with my older sister Annie and her husband, Buck Herring.

The idea of living in Los Angeles appealed to me. I would miss my brothers, but the draw of the big city won out. Nellie made the same choice, and so one day Buck and Annie came for us, and after we loaded our few personal belongings into the car trunk, we drove to LA together.

As we rolled down the highway, I had no idea that deciding to live with the Herrings would determine my life's career and even my spiritual direction. Nor did I have any idea how difficult living with Buck and Annie would be at times.

When I saw where Buck and Annie were living, I knew I'd made the right choice. Their house was cool—a hillside mansion in the heart of Hollywood that had been built by a silent-movie actress in the 1930s. The house's glory was fading, but I quickly grew to love it, not only because it was five times larger than the Sacramento place, but also because it had some fun features. The two-story house had a stucco exterior and was painted white throughout, having high, arched ceilings and arched doorways. Two spiral pillars rose to the living room ceiling, while three twelve-foot stained-glass windows adorned the entryway. (Although the house is long gone, you can still see the stained-glass windows on the cover of Barry McGuire's album *Seeds*. I wish I could have somehow kept those windows, which beautifully depicted grapevines.)

One other great feature of the house was the sun deck over the living room. I spent many hours there, enjoying incredible views of Hollywood and also daydreaming about the music and laughter from large parties that must have taken place in the house. I wondered which famous movie actors had pulled up in front in their fancy cars, exited with the help of a doorman, and walked gracefully to the front door.

Such Hollywood fantasy daydreams soon were replaced by the harsh reality that I was living in a very different world, with people who (through no fault of their own) had no idea how to raise two kids.

Buck and Annie were still newlyweds—married less than two years—when Nellie and I came to live with them. Annie was in her early twenties, Buck his early thirties, and—*zap*—an instant family with a pretty teenage girl and an untamed preteen boy. This was going to take some work. Buck and I were going to have some rough going for a long time.

For starters, I was terrified of the guy. Buck was a big man—six foot four and 240 pounds—while I was just a skinny kid. And we saw eye to eye on nothing. Our backgrounds and outlooks were completely different. He came from a family with one other sibling, while I came from one with eight other brothers and sisters. He had been brought up with discipline but little love. I had experienced the exact opposite.

The first clash came over my table manners. Before this, I had never thought twice about the way I ate, but Buck sure noticed. I had a nasty habit of smacking my food when I chewed, which drove him up a wall. He would ask me why I did it, and I would tell him that it made the food taste better. (It actually does—experiment yourself.) He tried different methods to end my bad habit—nothing worked. Finally, he just couldn't stand the smacking noise any longer, and one morning he made me sit outside by myself while I ate breakfast. It took a long time, but I finally broke the habit, and Buck could enjoy his meals again.

The other thing that was hard to come to grips with was that Annie was now my mom, so to speak. I suppose I should have felt some comfort that my sister would be there for me, but I really didn't know her. Before I was old enough to interact meaningfully with people, Annie had been out of the house making a life of her own in Los Angeles. So when I moved to LA, I instantly had—in addition to an overbearing mountain of a man trying to be a father figure—a newlywed sister I hardly knew trying out motherhood.

No wonder I mostly kept to myself the first few weeks after the move. I was trying to get a feel for my new life. It was strange to wake up in the morning and not see the smoke trailing off my dad's cigarette or have one of my older brothers giving me a hard time. And I still really missed my mom.

I sensed that beginning a new life with Buck and Annie was hard for Nellie too.

She was fourteen—a hard age for a girl even if everything in her life is normal. Nellie was starting to come into her own as a young lady, and I think the idea of Annie as Mom was overwhelming to her. What was it like for Nellie to wrestle with those things that a daughter might share with a mom but not necessarily with an older sister?

Meanwhile, Nellie and I had our own problems. We often fought over nothing. Our fights were not just verbal; many times we would kick and punch at each other, often resulting in one or both of us getting hurt. Once Nellie raked her fingernails down my chest, leaving me with several bleeding gouges.

Shortly after I became a Christian (that story's in the next chapter), Nellie and I had a fight that ended with Nellie slapping me hard across the face. I saw red and slapped her back, then stalked out of her room. About twenty minutes later, I came out of my room at the same time Nellie was coming out of hers. We both were on our way to tell the other we were sorry. We met in the hallway and gave each other a hug. We never had another fight.

Contact Sports

Buck and I—that was still another matter. We tried to find common ground—things we could do together as guys. We played catch with a baseball. We also wrestled—increasingly often. When we wrestled, I had to give it my all since Buck was so much bigger. One day, while we were going at it, I accidentally did something to Buck's neck. I didn't think much about it at the time, but ever since then, Buck has been a regular at the chiropractor's office.

Buck liked to play football, too, and he figured this might be a sport we could play together. A group of guys from our church, most of them full-grown men, would meet in a park on weekends to play. Normally, I would just watch, but since Buck knew I was a fast runner, one day he decided I should play. I was thirteen or fourteen and very skinny. The thought of lining up against these men was terrifying. Some of them, in my mind, were the size of compact cars.

"These guys are going to kill me," I told Buck.

But he didn't listen. "Come out here and play," he said.

I only remember two things about the game. First, on most plays, after the ball was snapped, I was drilled into the ground by one of these giants, resulting in the wind being knocked out of me and cartoon birds circling my head. The other memory was being chosen to catch the football. I think the logic behind this decision was that no one on the opposing team would ever dream I would be a receiver. The ball was snapped; I ran my pattern, caught the ball, and started running upfield. Then someone tackled me out of nowhere—hit me so hard that all I could remember was pain. It felt like a house had fallen on me.

I didn't play football with them again. Their world was too big for me.

Banned Music

Before moving in with Buck and Annie, I'd listened to all kinds of popular music on the radio, but I was especially drawn to the Motown sound. I found that it was easy for me to mimic the soulful vocal moves. To me, Motown was far more interesting than anything the white groups were doing.

Without really realizing it, I had become crazy about singing. I'd sing along with anything—even the vacuum cleaner as it whirred back and forth across the carpet, changing its pitch. The washing machine? I harmonized as it oscillated. You could say I learned to sing harmony from household appliances.

Later I learned that my hearing was unusually acute. Using an oscillator in a studio, I found I could hear tones of up to eighteen thousand cycles. Most people can hear up to sixteen thousand cycles. This sensitivity

The One That Got Away

In my early days of living with Buck and Annie, I had little in common with Buck. There was, however, one activity we quickly began to share together—playing catch in the front yard.

Buck could really throw a baseball; even though we had decent gloves, there were times he'd throw the ball so hard, it would break blood vessels in my hand. I didn't care. I just kept on throwing; it was fun to have something we could enjoy together.

One day, while playing catch, I decided to put all I could into one of my throws. As I released the ball, I knew I'd lost control. Buck jumped as high as he could to catch the flying object, but it passed over his head, sailed clear across the street, and smashed through the window of an apartment building lobby. Freaked out, I turned and ran into our house.

Buck found me, exclaiming, "What are you doing?"

I thought for a second. "I didn't know what to do."

He couldn't believe my first reaction was to turn tail and hide. "What?" he asked, incredulous. "You don't think they'll be able to tell where the ball came from?"

We sat down later and talked it through: whenever I'd done

could be a drawback. I used to walk into department stores where they used super-high-frequency alarm systems and drop to my knees from the pain in my ears. No one else could even hear the sounds, but I would have to go out and sit in the car because my ears couldn't take it.

I also discovered that my lung capacity is exceptional. I guess God

---

something wrong before, I was afraid my dad would kill me, so my first reaction was to run. Buck gave me courage to face the situation. This time, we went together to talk to the apartment manager, who understandably wanted us to pay for the window. The bill was something like three hundred dollars!

I felt terrible, because back then we didn't have that kind of money. But Buck and I continued to play catch—only I became more careful with my high, hard throws.

As circumstances developed, Buck and I continued to live in close proximity, not just for the few years remaining until I became an adult, but for many years to come while we traveled together as part of Second Chapter of Acts. It would be untruthful for me to say that our relationship ever was an easy one. We remained very different people. For me, everything is emotional and outward; Buck is the opposite. We clashed constantly.

But I can say that we grew to appreciate each other's gifts and learned to coexist. Once I was an adult and married with children of my own, I appreciated more fully the sacrifice Buck and Annie had made by taking in my sister and me when we were young. Buck, too, over the years began to accept me more. Today, I'm pleased to say, our relationship is better than it's ever been.

made me for sounds and music. I'm an acoustic man, born to sing. So it's no wonder—perfectly natural—that from an early age I loved listening to the radio.

After moving in with Buck and Annie, however, I wasn't allowed to listen to secular music anymore. We were all new Christians, and I guess their idea was that the "evil" music might cause me to backslide.

Because Buck had been a DJ and had managed some rock bands before he became a Christian, he had been deeply involved in things that are often linked with that lifestyle, including smoking dope, womanizing, and the like. But I was just a kid and had none of those ties with pop music. For example, I really wanted a lava light. I simply thought they were fun to look at. But I wasn't allowed to have one, because the lamp reminded Buck and Annie of parties they had gone to and things that had happened there.

Music was just something I enjoyed—it had no negative connotations. Music made me feel good. It was inspiring and a great escape from the pain and grief in my life. Music seemed about the only thing that couldn't be taken from me. So when Buck laid down the no-radio-listening mandate, it didn't sit well. I know Buck was just trying to protect me, but at the time, I just didn't get it.

Digging My Own Grave

School and I never got along well. I was easily distracted and had a much better time making other kids in class laugh than I did studying. As I quickly learned, teachers didn't much like me disrupting their classes, so I often found myself in detention or visiting with the principal. I brought home the hated pink slips from my teachers that explained my crimes. I had to get those pink slips signed by a guardian.

Guess who got to sign the pink slips?

Buck was a firm believer in corporal punishment ("Spare the rod," etc.), so when I brought home one of these slips, Buck and I would talk over the offense. Then he would spank me so hard that he burst blood vessels in his hand. He also prayed with me after the disciplining, which I thought was good, because it showed that he wasn't just mad but really wanted the best for me.

One day when I was in seventh grade, after I arrived home with yet another pink slip, Buck tried a new strategy. He told me to go to my room and write down all the things I didn't like about myself—all the habits and attitudes I would like to see die. After some thought, I came up with quite a list of improvements I wanted the Lord to make on me.

When I finished, I brought what I had written to Buck. He didn't want to read my inventory, but he told me to bring it along and to follow him outside. We walked to a dirt corridor between our house and the neighbor's house. He handed me a shovel while he took a measuring tape and marked out a large rectangle. "I want you to stay out here until you dig a hole six feet long, three feet wide, and six feet deep," He said.

My first thought was, *Great, I'm digging my own grave. I'll get this hole dug and then he'll bury me in it. No one will ever hear from me again.* After Buck went back inside the house, I found some gloves and started digging.

I never worked so hard in all my life. I was only halfway done when I discarded the gloves because they were falling apart. At several points during my excavating, Buck came out with his measuring tape and informed me of how much further I had to go. I dug for a long time, and with the help of my blisters, I became painfully aware of how hard it is to throw dirt over your head while standing in a hole that is nearly six feet deep.

As I got close to finishing the dig, I set the shovel aside and lay down in the hole. The cool ground soothed my aching, sweaty body as I stared upward and watched clouds passing over my small window to the sky.

Many thoughts ran through my mind, none of them good. I imagined Buck clubbing me over the head and filling in the hole. I heard a small voice inside me whisper, *Just get up out of this hole and run away. You don't have to put up with this.* I answered, *Where would I run to?* At that moment, I remembered that my brother Irmen had told me that if I ever had a problem living with Buck and Annie, I could always live with him. I wasn't sure how I would get there—he lived nearly four hundred miles away—but as I lay there in my "grave," the idea of going to live with him, Betty, and my two other brothers sounded inviting.

I was just gathering up the courage to leave when Buck came out to see how the work was coming. He took his last measurements of the hole, and when he found that it was indeed six feet long, three feet wide, and six feet deep, he told me to climb out.

Standing near the edge of the hole, I thought, *This is an awesome beginning to an underground fort.* But then Buck snapped me out of my daydream. "Matt, I want you to take your list and put it in the hole," he said. "I want you to bury those things that you want to see removed." That's when I noticed he had brought out an additional shovel. "And I want to help you fill it back in."

So I threw my list of bad things I'd written about myself into the hole and picked up my shovel. We both filled in the hole I had just spent the better part of a day digging.

Not all my troubles with my behavior ended that day, but it was a major turning point. Thanks, Buck.

I learned so much from Annie too. Even though it felt strange, as I got to know her better, I allowed her to be both a sister and a mother figure in my life.

But there was still much I didn't understand. Like all this strange Christian talk. Buck and Annie were "new Christians"—what in the world did that mean? Hadn't we all been Christians for a long time? They would say things like, "We've been born again." I would think, *Man, these people are on some kind of trip,* and let it go at that.

I didn't know I would soon take the trip myself.

5

Prayers Answered

My mother and father raised all their children as Roman Catholics. Though my mother was devoted to the faith, my father attended our church, St. John Vianney in Rancho Cordova, California, only because my mom made him. All of us siblings attended the parochial school attached to St. John Vianney, and every Sunday we would sit in church as the priest said Mass in Latin.

More times than not, my father dozed off during church services. This was a problem because he snored something terrible. That left the rest of us with a dilemma: should we wake him or not? We didn't want to let him snore, but if we woke him, he usually did not know where he was for a second or two, and then he would make such a ruckus that the embarrassment was greater than if we had just let him snore.

Apart from the entertainment provided by my father's snoring, Mass didn't touch me much. I didn't understand a word of Latin, so to me the whole thing was mumbo jumbo. My favorite part of Mass was going up for the Eucharist, because when that happened, I knew the service was almost over. Still, I tried to be a good Catholic. I wasn't sure what that meant, but especially after my mother died, I did my best because I knew it was what she would have wanted.

Every few weeks we had to go to confession. This terrified me. I knew I must have done something I needed forgiveness for, but every time I went into the confessional, after saying the obligatory "Father, I have sinned, and it's been two weeks since my last confession," I would draw a blank. I couldn't for the life of me think of anything I needed the priest to absolve me of. More than once I made up stuff just so I could get the priest to dispense penance and be done with it. One time I told the priest about sticking a cherry bomb (a firecracker on steroids) into the exhaust pipe of an old lady's car. I never actually did this, but it sounded good. The trick was to come up with a sin that would satisfy the priest but would not be so heinous that you would be there all day reciting "Hail Marys" and "Our Fathers."

Even though I may not have understood much of what went on in the church, I had a strong sense of being in the right club, so to speak. In school, the nuns taught us the catechism, and they had a way of making us believe anything they said. I believed being in the Catholic Church was the only way you could get to heaven. To me, being a good Catholic meant going through the right rituals—praying the rosary, praying to the right saints, praying the Stations of the Cross, and so on. No one ever mentioned to me that I could have a real, ongoing relationship with God.

Even with all the (to me) meaningless ritual, as I looked upon the immense cross suspended from the ceiling of our church, with Christ nailed to it in a perpetual state of suffering, a powerful and lasting impression entered my mind—one I couldn't shake.

The Jesus Movement Comes Home

At the beginning of the 1970s, although the Jesus movement had not yet come to national attention, it was in full swing in California. Ted and Liz

Wise had started the Living Room in the Haight neighborhood of San Francisco. Arthur Blessitt was exhorting hippies on Hollywood's Sunset Strip to "turn on to Jesus." Lonnie Frisbee had joined Calvary Chapel in Costa Mesa and was evangelizing thousands of young people. The Christian World Liberation Front was operating on the Berkeley campus of the University of California, while Hal Lindsey was running the Jesus Christ Light and Power Company at UCLA.

I knew nothing about all this at the time, though I was soon to be drawn into it in a big way.

My sister Annie's friend and one-time boyfriend, Buck Herring, was an aspiring band promoter in our hometown of Sacramento. Buck was working as a DJ at a Top 40 radio station one day when he received a phone call from one of his band members. In a panic-stricken voice, the musician informed Buck that their drug supplier had "gotten religion" and was refusing to deal drugs anymore.

Intrigued, Buck tracked down the drug supplier and asked him what was going on. The new Christian told Buck that he had been filled with the Holy Spirit and urged Buck to come to church with him. Buck agreed, and at that church service he turned his life over to Jesus.

After his spiritual rebirth, Buck began praying for Annie to be saved. Then one day he sensed the Lord saying to him, *Go find her.* Buck drove to LA and found Annie living with the members of her singing group at the home of a famous songwriter, Jimmy Webb, who was hoping to launch the group onto the charts.

Buck told Annie what had happened to him and said that she needed to be born again. He also gave her a copy of *Good News for Modern Man,* the Bible in modern English. Then he prayed with her before going home, asking God to reveal Himself to her. Annie was stunned by it all, but she was interested.

Camp Iwannagohome

I got saved in 1971 at First Assembly of God Church in North Hollywood, California. Not long after my conversion, I was encouraged by Buck to go to one of the church's summer camps. I'd never done anything like that before and was more than a little apprehensive about it.

To this day, I don't feel comfortable around crowds of people I don't know (ironic, don't you think?), and back then I knew very few kids from the church. I guess that was the point of sending me to the camp though—to introduce me to an environment where I could get to know others my own age.

The idea worked somewhat. I got to know one girl named Patty. In fact, the only thing I recall about the bus ride to camp—a trip that took us several hours outside of Los Angeles to a location in the Sierra Nevada mountains—was making out with Patty, off and on, the whole way.

Once the bus parked and we filed out, we learned that we had a ten-mile hike to get to our camp. I was not, as they say, a happy camper when I heard that news. We hiked for what seemed an eternity. I know there must have been some kind of guide, or we would have all become lost, though I don't remember much in the way of camp leadership showing us the way. (Actually, some of our team did remain lost for several hours after the rest of us had made camp.)

There were a few times on our trek to camp when I would have sworn we were as lost as lost could be. About the time I started freaking out (of course, being a cool teenager, I never let on), we would come across someone from our group who would assure us that we were on the right track.

Just as my swearing reached its apex (at least under my breath), we came upon a beautiful mountain lake, and as I looked about, I began to see evidence that we had reached the camp. There wasn't much in the way of permanent structures; the camp was nothing more than a few tables and tents.

It didn't take long before just about every camp rule was broken—and I did more than my share. I was really growing to hate my church-camp experience. The water in the lake was so cold that it hurt your skin if you tried to get in. Some of the kids were acting like bullies, which I always hated. Girls would sneak into the guys' tents and fill our sleeping bags with pine needles, pine cones, and anything else that was lying around. That was great fun...not!

I forget what my trespass was, but I incurred the wrath of one of the camp leaders, who pulled me aside and told me he was seriously considering sending me home early. He backed down when I looked him in the eye and told him that "going home early sounded pretty good to me." He was going to have to come up with something better than that to rattle me.

The trip wasn't 100 percent bad. We did have a good "come to Jesus" meeting around the campfire one night, where I genuinely felt the presence of God. But other than that, I hated that camp experience. I never did go on another church camping trip.

Annie had been on a spiritual search ever since our mother had died, hoping to find a solution for her pain and grief. She had investigated various New Age–type beliefs and had tried "self-realization." But still, nothing in her life seemed worthwhile—not the religious alternatives, not the drugs, not even the possibility of fame.

Now she picked up the Bible that Buck had left her and began reading it from the back. In the book of Revelation she found an image of Jesus Christ she had never encountered before. It made sense to her. He was the King of kings and Lord of lords, and she needed to follow Him.

Annie's conversion came about not long before we learned my father was dying of leukemia. She drove up to Sacramento and asked him if he wanted to receive Jesus into his heart. There was no resistance at all; he said, "Oh, yes." The first thing he did after receiving the Lord was to pray for his children, asking that they would come to know Jesus too. And in that way, at the end of his life, his prayers were united with my mother's for our salvation.

After my father died and I moved to Los Angeles, Buck and Annie tried to get me to go to the church they'd attended since getting married— First Assembly of God Church in North Hollywood. I had major issues with this. To me, if you attended any church other than a Catholic church, you were asking to burn forever in the fiery pits of hell. The Catholic Church was the only church God would recognize; every other denomination was heretical.

Struggling with these issues, I reluctantly started attending Buck and Annie's church. I felt a sense of fear, betrayal, and guilt for not going to a Catholic church, but Buck and Annie kept reassuring me that it was okay.

The Sunday services at the Assembly of God church were completely different from what I was used to. The first time I went, I kept waiting for signals to kneel or to stand or to file up for Communion. Those signals never came. Instead, I heard a man preaching things I'd never heard before.

It took a couple of weeks for me to feel more comfortable at this new church. I would sit back and watch the people in the service to see if they were any different from people outside the church. I had to know there was more power in believing the way these people did than in believing what I had been raised with. I wasn't about to jump ship without seeing the reality of what this new preacher was talking about.

One Sunday, while the minister was giving his message, I felt something I'd never felt before. For the first time, I got a glimpse of why Christ had suffered. Growing up, I knew of the sufferings of Christ, but I never had understood what they meant. The focus had been on the fact that Christ had suffered for me, but never on the reason why. I knew little of the redemptive aspects of Christ's sufferings.

While the preacher preached, I became more and more conscious of a God who had died for me. I heard about the blood of Christ, how it alone had the power to cleanse me from sin. I saw sin for the first time as the thing that was keeping me from walking with God like I'd always wanted to, even as a small child. The Holy Spirit of God was calling me to Christ. What was I going to do with this new insight?

The preacher, at the close of his sermon, gave a compelling altar call. I walked to the front to receive Jesus.

Nellie had become a Christian the week before. Now, for the first time since we had moved in with Buck and Annie, we were all on the same page—spiritually at least.

Around the time of my conversion, Annie and Buck started having what we called the "Tuesday night prayer meetings" at our house. Usually Buck headed them up. These meetings involved more than Bible study. We began the evenings with a shared meal, then gathered in the living room to sing songs. This was followed by prayer and Scripture reading. All of us were new Christians, hungry for anything of the Lord we could get our hands on.

On more than one occasion, the Lord showed up so powerfully that people were healed of all kinds of maladies. Being new Christians, we would read things in the Word about Christ healing people, and how we would do even greater things, and we simply believed it. So when people had physical complaints, we asked God to heal, and He did. I saw legs lengthen, colds disappear, earaches vanish—on and on it went.

As I said, we always served food before the prayer meeting. And because the family didn't have a lot of money, Annie was always concerned there wouldn't be enough. Before anyone showed up, Buck, Annie, Nellie, and I would pray that the Lord would make the food stretch far enough to feed everyone who came that night.

One night more people than usual filled the house. We looked at each other and said, "Well, I guess we'll just keep serving the food until it runs out." But something bizarre happened: people came back for seconds and thirds, but the pot of food just wouldn't empty. We even had leftovers!

Some months Buck and Annie didn't have enough money for the rent. The old Hollywood mansion was perfect for the growing number of people attending the Tuesday night prayer meetings; God wouldn't want us to lose it, would He? We would pray, and the next day there would be money on our fireplace mantel.

Those evenings of Bible study, fellowship, and prayer to this day remain some of the greatest developmental times of my Christian walk. I learned in that old mansion that God still performs miracles. I didn't know enough not to simply believe what God said. And He showed up with such power that it made me all the more hungry to know Him in a deeper and more intimate way.

A friend of the family, Albie Pearson, when talking years later about the Jesus movement, said, "The Spirit of God was so strong that you could burp with the anointing." It was a good thing that the power of God was so evident; later in my life there would be times when I would need to remember something that strong to hold on to.

Feeling the Power

I had been a Christian for a number of weeks when a traveling evangelist came to our church and preached about the "baptism of the Holy Spirit." I had heard about this, but it sounded spooky to me. There was a lot of "tongue talking" in our church, and this fascinated me. I knew some of these people, and they seemed levelheaded. So I wondered why they were involved in what seemed like some kind of weird voodoo.

As the preacher explained about speaking in tongues and what it meant to be "filled with the Holy Ghost," I thought, *Man, what is this guy smoking?* The struggle I faced was the fact that, up to this point anyway, the people at this church had always told me the truth. They had introduced me to Jesus—I knew that was right. They had told me I could walk with Him—I had found that to be true as well. Now they had this preacher telling me about all this wacky tongue-talking stuff. It didn't make sense.

At the end of the service, I decided that even though I had no clue what this guy was talking about, I would go down front and find out what all the hoopla was about.

As the evangelist made his rounds, laying hands on different people, I could hear them speaking all this *"Shaba de doobe doo la la shawndie re bo bo"* stuff. Again I was thinking, *This is some kinda weird!* The evangelist finally came, laid his hands on me, and said, "Just take some deep breaths. Let the words come from deep within you." Before long the *"Shala la la dobie do condo bo greepa"* talk was tumbling off my tongue. "You've got it, brother," the evangelist said. "Don't you feel the power?"

I kept it up for as long as the man stood in front of me, but as soon as he moved on to his next victim (that's how I felt about it at the time), I quit with the mumbo-jumbo talk and went back to my seat. Annie and Buck asked if I had received a new language. I looked at them and said, "Yeah, I think so." I didn't have the heart to tell them I thought the whole thing was nonsense.

On the ride home after the service, the questions rolled around in my heart and mind. *Why do these people, who are relatively normal, buy into this strange behavior? Did I really speak in tongues, or was it just made-up gobbledygook?* I asked the Lord to show me the truth.

No sooner had I asked the question than I began to feel something I'd never felt before. An overwhelming sense of God's presence came over me. I began to speak in tongues involuntarily, and tears streamed down my face. This went on for about a half hour. The power of God was so gargantuan that my questions disappeared and I had no doubt of His sovereignty.

Churches Along the Way

The four of us worshiped at First Assembly of God for about a year before joining the Church on the Way in Van Nuys, pastored by Jack Hayford. This church has since become big and influential, but at the time there were only about sixty people attending. Buck was producing a record for Pat Boone, who attended the church and invited us.

Over the next decade, until we moved to Texas, the Church on the Way remained our church home. In Texas I worshiped mostly with small congregations—Community Christian Fellowship and Prairie Creek Baptist Church. After moving to Colorado, we worshiped for some years at

New Life Church in Colorado Springs, a megachurch under the leadership of Ted Haggard. Now we enjoy the more intimate and contemplative worship of an Anglican church near our home. In some ways, this latest gathering of believers has brought me full circle to some of the best aspects of my Roman Catholic heritage.

Through the years, I've had some disappointments in the church. I bear some scars for treatment I've received or observed by people acting in Christ's name. But while some in the church have let me down, just as, I'm sure, I've offended others at times, Jesus Christ has always been faithful to me.

I'll never forget the image of that bleeding Man who hung on the crucifix in the Catholic church of my childhood. He suffered and died not only so I could be born again but also to carry me through all that I would encounter in life. This phrase is in a song I wrote and recorded:

I understand my mother's heart for me,
wanting Jesus to make me all that I could be.

What I had in mind when I wrote that song titled "Love" was a time in my childhood when I barged in on my mom and found her on her knees praying. Somehow, I knew that she was praying for me. And there's no question that for a long time, perhaps especially in those later years when she was invaded by poor health, she prayed fervently for her children. She wanted us to know the Lord.

Those prayers all were answered, as one by one, I and all my siblings came to follow Jesus.

6

School Days

To my disappointment, I'm sure, I learned that even in Hollywood, kids my age had to go to school.

After moving to Los Angeles, Nellie and I registered for public school. We had attended a parochial school in Sacramento. Public school in the big city? I wasn't sure I was ready for this.

Buck took me to meet the principal of what we thought would be my new elementary school. The principal glanced at my records and said, "At your age, you should be going into junior high, not sixth grade."

"Yeah, I know. My mom made me repeat first grade," I answered.

"Would you be willing to give seventh grade a shot?" the principal asked.

I thought, *Why not? One less year of school—I'm all for that.*

So, with the principal's recommendation, in the blink of an eye I went straight from fifth grade to seventh grade. How cool—I was thrashing the system! I had flunked first grade and now was going to skip sixth—how many people can do that? In September I entered seventh grade at LeConte Junior High School in Los Angeles.

I had never been what you would call a lover of school, but all of a sudden I was in a situation I simply couldn't handle. In particular, by skipping sixth grade, I missed out on some math fundamentals. I went from adding and subtracting to doing algebra overnight. I have never been so utterly lost at anything in my life. They tried putting me in an easier math class, but the teacher was so lame that it didn't help much. It was a disaster. And Buck wearing out his hand on my south side didn't help.

School had always been hard time for me. I always heard things like, "If you would just apply yourself" or "I don't think you're paying attention in class." I admit it was easier for me to blame the teachers for my problems than myself. Nellie did well in school, but for me it was like pulling teeth.

For some reason, I just couldn't grasp some of the simplest building blocks of education. For instance, to this day I don't know my multiplication tables—what's 8 x 9?—hand me a calculator. How frustrating was that? I could practice with flashcards until I saw double, but the answers never stuck in my head. About the time I'd think I was making headway, I would try again the next day and could not remember.

Buck tried to help and worked with me on my multiplication tables, but after countless sessions, he gave up in frustration.

I wasn't dyslexic—reading was never a problem. For me, it was numbers that drove me crazy. I couldn't figure out what was wrong and even worried that I might be mentally retarded.

Because of my inability to work with numbers, I avoided situations that might show my deficiencies. I wouldn't play card games that required quick calculations. It took many years before I no longer cared who knew about my deficiencies. I stopped trying to do things I was no good at. Instead, I surrounded myself with people who could help me with the things I couldn't do well. (Today, for example, my wife handles all the money matters in our household.) Don't ask me to balance a checkbook. But do you want me to sing harmony on a song or help produce a CD? I learned to focus on my strong points.

Hollywood Professional School

By the fall of 1972, Second Chapter of Acts was touring quite a bit, and Buck thought it might be good for Nellie and me to get out of the normal public school system. I had survived seventh and eighth grade—or was it that the school had survived me? I suppose Buck knew ninth grade would not be a pretty picture for me, so he enrolled both Nellie and me in Hollywood Professional School, which catered to kids who were involved in acting, singing, or some other activity that required shorter school days. This school, which closed its doors in 1985 after fifty years of operation (I don't think I was responsible!), listed many famous performers among its alums, including Judy Garland, Mickey Rooney, Betty Grable, John Barry-more Jr., Annette Funicello, and Valerie Bertinelli.

Studying with the rich and famous wasn't my favorite thing about the school; I liked the short day in classes. I arrived at 9:00 a.m., and school was out by 12:30 p.m. The school was little more than a place to pick up your homework for the night. We had classes, but they were so short that about the time the teacher got into a subject, the bell rang and we scrambled to the next class. The quality of education at Hollywood Professional was less than stellar. My math teacher was half as old as dirt and some years before had suffered a stroke that affected her left side. I'm not poking fun at her—it was just that math was my toughest subject, and now I had a teacher who wouldn't explain things during class, who wouldn't help me after school, and whose speech was so slurred I couldn't understand half of what she was saying.

It was almost impossible not to stare at her. She would take her paralyzed left arm, give it a couple of swings, prop it against the blackboard, and then with her good hand take the math book and stuff it up against her bad arm so she could write the problems. After she had finished putting

63

the assigned problems on the chalkboard, she sat down in her chair and ignored us until the bell rang for next period.

My Spanish teacher seemed crazy as a loon. She taught both Spanish and French, actually, but it was obvious that she loved French and was indifferent to Spanish. Her French class ended right before we arrived for Spanish, and I remember walking into her class early a few times, only to see her erasing an elaborate French lesson. She hardly ever used the chalkboard when teaching Spanish; she'd just explain a few things verbally and have us work on lessons from our book. She seemed to always be going on and on about one student or another in her French class, or she would wish out loud that she had a Spanish student like so-and-so from her French class.

She had a special dislike for me, and the feeling was mutual. One day she needed to step out of the room for a few moments. As soon as she left, several friends and I ran to the bathroom and soaked paper towels in the sink. We returned to the classroom and threw the wadded up towels as hard as we could against the chalkboard. The soaked paper left some interesting shapes as it slammed into the board. Before the teacher made it back, we had covered nearly every square inch of that chalkboard as well as much of the surrounding wall.

As you can imagine, when she walked in and saw her board covered with wet paper wads, she went off. She yelled so hard that I thought she would have a stroke and end up like the math teacher. After she threatened us with everything she could think of, trying to get somebody to fess up, she realized we weren't going to budge. She finally made some of us take the remainder of class time to clean up the mess. It was a small price to pay.

A few weeks later, this teacher called me up to her desk, where she informed me under her breath that I had earned an F in her class. She then told me, with an uncharacteristic growl, that she was giving me a D just so she wouldn't have to see me again.

When I attended Hollywood Professional School, students like Judy Garland and Mickey Rooney were long gone. But some celebrity kids were attending the school. I got to know Christopher Knight—Peter on television's *The Brady Bunch*—pretty well.

What Beatles?

Hollywood Professional School was for young performers, but one boy I met there knew nothing about music, and he didn't act. Why was he there? Maybe he was one of those kids whose parents had more money than God and didn't feel comfortable sending their "precious" to public school. Anyway, this guy had caught my attention because of the volume of things he knew absolutely nothing about.

One day, when talking to him, I happened to mention the Beatles, and he said that he had never heard of them. This was the early seventies, remember. Every other person I knew could have named all four members of the Beatles. Yet here was a kid trying to convince me that he had never even heard of the band.

"That's impossible," I said to him. "Have you been living in a bubble?" But he kept telling me it was true.

So I'd sing part of a Beatles song for him, and then I'd say, "Have you heard that one?" He would say no. I'd sing another, but he just kept up with his claim of not recognizing any of the tunes.

I've never in all my life been so amazed at the possibility that someone living in Los Angeles—not in a grass hut in some rainforest—had never heard of the Beatles!

Maureen McCormick, who played Marcia on the same show, also went to the school, but I never got to know her because she was in a higher grade. It took me a while to warm up to Christopher, because I didn't want to be one of those kids who bugged him. But in the end my winning personality shone through, and we got to talking. I guess I expected him to be stuck up, but Christopher was nice—so down to earth. We never developed a relationship outside of school, but I understood he had a busy schedule.

One girl at school was the daughter of an opera singer, and she told me she was in training to become an opera singer herself. (I can't remember her name, though I can easily recall her fair skin and bright red hair.) I asked her to sing me something, and she sang a few notes of an opera she was working on. I was impressed. Her voice was as big as all outdoors. I thought it was weird to meet a girl my age who actually *wanted* to sing opera, but she certainly had a voice for it.

Many years later I was watching a show on PBS in which a conductor was leading a classical piece, when all of a sudden the camera panned over to a red-headed woman standing in front of a microphone. The next thing I heard was her voice. It had matured, but I could tell by the tone and sheer volume that it was Old Red busting a gut. How cool—and strange, too—to see her onstage fulfilling her childhood dream.

Education by Mail

Throughout my school career, teachers made all the difference to me. If they made a subject interesting, I found it much easier to pay attention and retain information. But most of the teachers at Hollywood Professional School seemed to be just punching the clock.

I attended there for two years. (Nellie went there for one year before starting at Hollywood High.) It had become clear that Second Chapter of Acts was going to be around for a while and that a good deal of touring was still in my future. So Buck arranged for me to get the rest of my education through a correspondence school out of Chicago.

The school would send assignments to me; I would send homework back and get my grades. And that was that. I did some of my homework on the bus and the rest of it during the winter season when we stayed home. I didn't enjoy it, but to me it seemed like an easy way to complete the requirement that every kid had to finish school. What I didn't clearly recognize at the time was that not having face-to-face contact with teachers, even lousy ones, meant that my education was even more deficient than before. Even with Buck and Annie giving advice and encouragement on my homework, I lacked the motivation, not to mention the personal instruction, that would have been provided by a teacher in the classroom.

I kept up with my correspondence classes into my senior year of high school, but then I quit while I was still a few credits shy of graduating. At the time it didn't seem like a big deal; I was traveling and making music—the homework was just getting in the way of doing what I liked. What difference did it make if I had a degree? Since then, though, not finishing my schooling has become one of the greatest regrets of my life.

It's a good thing that touring with Second Chapter of Acts was a learning experience in itself. While I can't quickly tell you what twelve times seven equals or always vouch for my spelling, I learned a lot about what life was like in America and in many foreign nations, how to make music, and how to minister to people in the Lord's name.

7

First Notes

That my sisters and I could make music at all is something of a miracle.

It started with Annie. Buck bought her a piano as a wedding present. He knew she was musically gifted, so even though Annie had never played the piano before, he found an old upright for fifty dollars (half the ivories were missing, and the rest were yellowed) and brought it home.

With Buck working long days and with Nellie and me off at school, Annie had quite a few hours to herself each day. She would sit down at the piano and experiment, plunking out simple melodies, then adding chords. That's how she learned to play the piano; she never had a lesson.

Annie began to write her own songs, little tunes that expressed the feelings of awe and affection she felt toward Jesus. At first she asked Buck to write the words to her songs—Annie was confident in making up melodies but felt inadequate with lyrics. He did this for a while, but Annie was writing a new song or more every day, and he couldn't keep up. Finally he told her, "Let the message God has placed in your heart just come out in words."

So that's what she did. Annie has always called herself a "song receiver," not a songwriter. She just wrote down what the Lord shared with her.

In the fall of 1970, Nellie and I would come home from LeConte Junior High in the middle of the afternoon. Like most kids, I guess, we had an after-school snack and then pulled up chairs beside Annie at the piano and listened to her new songs. Who could have predicted what was about to happen? Certainly not me—I liked music but knew nothing about how to blend a song with others. We never stopped and discussed how we might harmonize a song. We just sat around that old beat-up piano singing the notes that came naturally and felt good. Nellie and I watched Annie's head bobbing, her hands smacking the keyboard as we flowed together in rhythm and harmony, guessing with uncanny accuracy where the music was going next, landing our parts as we went along.

I'm sure the singing helped us express the grief we still felt after losing our parents. At that point, maybe especially for Nellie and me, singing together as siblings was a time of healing, a time to think about something other than being orphaned. I know I still had an ache and emptiness in my heart. I missed Mom and Dad as well as my brothers.

It's a hard thing to explain—the music, the way it could make us feel so much better. When we harmonized, something magical happened. Even though just a kid, I sensed that the whole (we three singing together) was much bigger than our individual parts. At the time I really didn't understand that what I was feeling was the presence of God's Spirit.

We were such new Christians that we didn't understand what was happening spiritually. At times, while we were singing, tears would stream down my face. Sometimes I saw visions when we sang that way together. The Spirit of the Lord would fall so heavily some days that we would stop and take stock of what the Lord was revealing. Those sessions of worship became wonderfully powerful to me because, for the first time, I saw the Lord as a living God who showed up as my heart was poured out before Him.

Looking back now, a part of me wishes we'd had a tape recorder going to capture some of those moments. There were so many beautiful little choruses that came from that place of worship, but for the most part, we looked at them as something private, songs that were sung "unto the Lord," as opposed to songs that were meant to be recorded and shared with the public. Nevertheless, besides our own worship and healing, the notion grew among us that maybe God wanted to use our music for more than just our personal well-being.

As I mentioned before, Annie, Nellie, and I never intended to become a group that would perform in public. For one thing, you would have been hard pressed to find three people more insecure and shy about performing. We couldn't believe that people would want to listen to *us* sing. But some of our friends heard us singing Annie's songs at home, and this led to what we believed was God calling us to sing a few times at coffeehouses located in churches and that sort of thing.

Even in such small venues, we were scared to death. Each time, I had vicious stage fright—rapid heartbeat, sweaty palms, a sick feeling in my stomach. It took all of our combined courage to get up there and start a song. But once the music started and we began to harmonize, the anxiety passed. It was almost like we were back home, sitting around the old piano making music for our King. We got into it, and so did those listening.

Audiences responded kindly in those early days. But still, if someone had told me that in a few years we would be singing our little songs to thousands of people across America, I would have fallen out of my chair laughing.

Barry

I've already told the story of how Nellie and I were wakened by the sound of loud music one night and came downstairs to sing for Barry McGuire. I don't know if it was that night or sometime later when Buck suggested that we (Second Chapter) could sing background vocals on Barry's record.

Barry thought that was a wonderful idea, and a long-term relationship was born.

Barry's first Christian record was called *Seeds.* We had already recorded a few songs, including "I'm So Happy," on a contract that Pat Boone had helped us arrange with MGM. (That project never led to a complete album.) But *Seeds* was the first recording project where I got to really observe what was going on. The process was a joy.

I loved going to the studio for recording sessions. I would try my best not to get into anybody's hair, but the procedures of recording were so much fun that it was all I could do not to be a nuisance. As the musicians prepared themselves (tuning up, placing microphones properly, setting sound levels, and so on), I would sneak out into the studio and find a spot where I was out of the way but still close enough to watch their every move. I loved to hear the players play in the studio, as opposed to being in the control room, where I'd have to listen through the monitors. I was fascinated by how these guys interacted musically.

Barry's album was Second Chapter's first real recording opportunity, even if we just sang backgrounds. We got along so well with Barry that creating parts for each of the songs hardly seemed like work.

I knew from then on that I would always love doing background vocals. It requires a lot of creativity. You start with nothing and end up with harmony parts that intertwine around each other, complementing the lead singer.

Once Barry's album was finished, he wanted to take the music on the road. That meant we needed a band.

Up to this point, our "performances" had been before Christian audiences in coffeehouses and the like with just the three of us singing around a piano—certainly never with a full band. Appearing with Barry would be a whole different deal. Since he had been a popular singer in the secular arena before being born again, his followers were still largely non-Christians. How would a secular audience react to sisters and a brother singing new songs about Jesus?

A band would certainly help. We recruited some musicians from Torrance who lived together on Node Street, so we called them the "Node Gang." They were incredibly good.

Our first concert with Barry was set for Church of the Open Door in Los Angeles. Second Chapter of Acts would sing background for Barry, as well as do a set of our own songs with the Node Gang.

Waiting backstage, my sisters and I were scared out of our skin. For Barry, performing in front of a large audience was routine. Not for us! We were so freaked that none of us even remembers what we wore that night, but since it was 1973 and the hippie thing was still going down, I'm sure there was a tie-dye fashion moment or two.

We calmed our fears and walked onstage to some scattered hand claps. We began to sing Annie's songs, and the butterflies flew off. It was like old times around the beat-up piano back at the Hollywood mansion—"Easter Song," "Love, Peace, Joy," "I Fall in Love," and "I'm So Happy."

I'll never forget the audience reaction after we finished our first song, "Going Home." As the music died away, I hoped to hear at least polite applause, but at first it was dead silent. *Great. They think we're absolutely terrible,* I thought. Then someone began to clap and others joined in—but it was low key, almost respectful—for sure no cheering and foot stomping. After the concert some people said the reason they didn't applaud at first was because they were so affected by the music that they didn't know how to react.

Our second concert was held at the Sacramento Memorial Auditorium in our old hometown. We played there because our song "I'm So Happy" was charting in the top five on the local secular radio station where Buck had once been the program director. He had also put on large concerts in the area, so Sacramento seemed a good choice.

We were still experimenting, and for this concert Buck thought it might be a good idea to locate the band in front of the singers. So we stood on small risers so people could still see us. That didn't work out well soundwise and probably looked odd, so we never tried that again. Of course the crowd didn't know any of our music—except "I'm So Happy," which after much whooping, clapping, and whistling we sang at least four times in a row!

The drummer in the Node Gang couldn't make the first few gigs, so we hired a Los Angeles studio drummer named David Kemper. (David later played with Jerry Garcia and Bob Dylan.) After those first concerts, David suggested we get into a studio and record an album. That led to our first recording, *With Footnotes,* in April of 1974.

We toured with the Node Gang for a year or so, playing in different U.S. locations as well as New Zealand. Unfortunately, we didn't see eye to eye spiritually with some of the players in the band, so we had to conclude our musical relationship. The group went on to some notoriety as a secular band named The Call.

Billy Ray

Our experiences on the road with Barry McGuire were so good that we knew we needed to get more aggressive with our own recording and touring. The first complete album Second Chapter recorded was for Myrrh Records, a label of Word Records in Texas. Billy Ray Hearn was the president of Myrrh. He had first heard us sing in 1973 when we were traveling with Jimmy Owens doing his musical *Come Together*—in which we did step-out solos as part of the choir. Later we met with Billy Ray backstage after our concert at Baylor University, but Buck's first impression of Billy Ray wasn't favorable. He thought Billy Ray was too "frisky."

After producing Barry's album, Buck had tried to shop it to several secular labels. The industry people liked Barry's album but had no idea how they would market music with such a strong Christian theme. To them it was easier to market the old Barry than this new, cleaned-up version.

At that point Buck remembered Billy Ray, and because there were no other Christian labels willing to promote those of us who had a more contemporary bent, he gave Billy Ray a call. In their phone conversation Buck asked, "How much would you pay for the best album you've ever heard?" That piqued Billy Ray's interest.

Billy Ray flew to Los Angeles to meet with Buck and listened to Barry's record. Billy liked it, and while he was there, Buck played for him some of the music Second Chapter had recorded for MGM. He was really taken by

Potted Plants

When I was about fifteen years old, Second Chapter had a tour that included a stop in Sacramento. We worked it so that we had a day off there before the concert. I opted to stay with my brothers while other members of my family stayed with other relatives in the area.

Not long after Nellie and I had moved to LA, my brothers had started growing and smoking marijuana. I wasn't at the house long before my brother Jack said, "Matt, have you ever tried pot?"

(continued on the next pages)

"No, I've never had much of an opportunity to," I replied.

"Well, I'm going to have some in the backyard if you want to join me," Jack said. He grabbed his bag of dope and a pipe and headed out. Out back I watched as he stuffed his pipe and lit up. Not long after taking a couple of hits, he was laughing away. He looked at me and said, "Do you want to take a hit?"

At first I said no. I was thinking, *Buck would kill me.* But my brother kept prodding and saying things like, "This stuff won't hurt you" and "I'll never tell a soul." So I figured that if I was ever going to try it, this was the safest place to do so.

"Pass the pipe," I told him and grabbed the lighter. I lit the weed and took a huge hit. I waited a few minutes and told him I felt absolutely nothing.

"Here, take another hit," he said.

I took another big hit and waited a few more minutes.

Jack asked, "You feel it yet?"

"No."

By this time my brother was so stoned that he was looking at me in disbelief, laughing his guts out at me. (I found out later that when you're a first-time smoker, it takes a lot for you to get high.) After I'd taken my third hit, I began thinking there must be something wrong with me.

The next thing I knew, the dope hit me over the head like a brick. The whole backyard began spinning, and I thought, *I might have smoked a bit too much.* The sensation was stronger than I had expected. I looked at Jack and said, "Okay, I definitely feel it now."

He just started laughing, and this time I laughed with him.

Just as I was trying to get used to the feeling of being stoned, which I wasn't so sure I liked, someone showed up at the front door. I instantly began thinking, *How am I going to explain this? Man, I'm so busted. What was I thinking?*

"It's cool," Jack said. "Just sit tight, and I'll find out who it is."

As I sat in the backyard waiting, I realized how paranoid the stuff makes you. I thought, *It's the cops! I just know it's the cops!* The unlikelihood of cops dropping by for a visit was something I didn't take into account; I just knew it had to be them. I had visions of being hauled off to jail and having to explain my actions to Buck.

After a few moments, Jack came back out where I was, accompanied by a guy about my age. At first I didn't recognize him. Then as he began to speak, I realized it was my friend Don, who I hadn't seen in some years. Don sat down with us and asked how things were with me. We conversed for a few minutes, catching up on old times, and then he asked if I was still into that "Jesus thing."

Those words cut right into my soul. Through my fog, I tried my best to assure him I was still very much into that "Jesus thing." I felt terrible. I could hear the Holy Spirit saying, *This isn't what I had in mind when I asked you to be ready in and out of season.*

Gratefully, Don couldn't stay long, as I was finding it nearly impossible to act straight while he was there.

That experience put an end to my experimentation with drugs. A few years later, by the grace of God, all but one of my brothers had quit their pot habits and become strong Christians.

what he heard, so Buck felt it might be good for Billy Ray to hear some of our newer songs. The three of us gathered around the piano and sang. There always was an intangible thing that happened when we'd pour our hearts out in such a simple way. Billy Ray's eyes began to sparkle with love for what he was hearing. It didn't take us long to realize that we needed someone like Billy Ray in our corner.

Once we got to know Billy Ray, we fell in love with the guy. We signed with Myrrh Records and recorded our first complete album—*With Footnotes*—with Billy Ray. That album contained one of the most popular songs Second Chapter ever recorded: "Easter Song." I get a kick out of seeing that song in many of today's hymnals. There is my sister's name, included among the ranks of such writers as Isaac Watts. (I haven't gotten there yet as a writer, but I'm not done yet!)

We stayed with Billy Ray for many years. We even left Myrrh to join Billy Ray in his adventure of starting a new label called Sparrow Records. As a matter of fact, the first record Sparrow released was Annie's first solo album, called *Through a Child's Eyes* (1976). Billy Ray always had a sharp business mind. And through the years, even after we were no longer on his label, there were times when Buck would call Billy Ray to ask him a business question, and Billy Ray would always give Buck a straight-up answer, even if it wasn't in Billy Ray's best financial interests.

Pioneers

Along with Larry Norman, Love Song, and a number of other artists, Second Chapter was a part of the early "Jesus music" scene. What would later become known as contemporary Christian music was in its formative stages as our group launched. We were pioneers, although we didn't know it at the time.

The reaction of listeners to our music in the early days was often something like, "Wow! That was really new and fresh!" But getting that kind of response was never our intent. We weren't trying to be clever or seeking to be pioneers. We just wanted to work on our own sound and do what we felt God was calling us to do. I'm proud when people say that we had a distinctive sound. Maybe our unique harmony came in part from our sibling genetics. We were just trying to be ourselves, not copy anybody else.

Entertainment was not our primary goal. True, we paid a lot of attention to creating good music, but we took even more seriously our responsibility to represent Jesus well. And I think that's really why people responded so well to us: they were touched by the spiritual dynamic of what God was doing through us.

In the end, I think our insecurity was good for us. It kept us humble and helped us focus on God instead of ourselves. We knew we were good singers, but we didn't get big heads because we had achieved something or arrived somewhere.

Second Chapter of Acts was never about us and our abilities; it was about Jesus. And He was pleased to use us for seventeen years.

8

On Tour (and On Tour and On Tour)

In 1974 when our first album, *With Footnotes,* hit the street, we hit the road.

Our first tours were grueling, to say the least. When we left LA in our little shuttle bus, we often were gone for eight weeks straight. We took one day off a week to do laundry—and often traveled on the same day to the next concert destination. Some of the cities were just too far apart to travel and perform a concert on the same day.

"Easter Song" was getting a lot of attention, which for us as an unknown group, helped make booking concerts easier and gave sponsors something they could push in radio spots and the like. But even with one song that people liked, we knew it would take much time and effort to make touring work. Oh, were we right about that.

Some of the band guys and I ended up calling travel days "Beelzebus." Being trapped in that tiny bus for days on end was the closest thing I could relate to hell at the time. During one tour I was on the road so long that I literally could not remember what day of the week it was. And maybe worse, I couldn't recall the month either.

During most of the years Second Chapter of Acts was together, in January we would gather to pray and try to discern God's intentions for the group during the coming year. Twice we determined that we needed to take a year off from touring. The first time was in 1976, when we all sensed that being Second Chapter of Acts had begun to overwhelm our being a family. During that twelve-month break, we gave attention to our priorities and straightened out our relationships with one another, as well as did some recording. The second hiatus came in 1983 when we felt the Lord wanted us to rest. During that year we built our new facility in Lindale, Texas. And it was in that year that I married.

We stayed busy for the better part of two decades. Normally we toured in the spring and fall and cut records in the off season. Second Chapter of Acts ended up recording sixteen albums and performed close to two thousand concerts. We toured America, Canada, New Zealand, Australia, and Western Europe.

By the time I was sixteen years old, I had traveled to every state in the Union except Alaska. Touring as much as we did became so much a part of my life that I never thought of what I was missing, the experiences that normal kids my age were having. To me, what I was doing was normal. And to this day I have no regrets about the choice I made to tour with Second Chapter. What I saw and experienced outweighs anything I might have missed by being on the road.

Host Families and Hotels

Touring as hard as we did started to pay off, not so much in the money department, but because after a few years we got to the point where we could stay in hotels instead of people's homes. Don't misunderstand me.

I'm grateful for the hospitality so many people showed us. But I can't begin to tell you how old it got to have to stay up after concerts and chat amiably with host families. How many times can you be asked, "What's it like to be onstage?" and not want to strangle someone?

When you are on the road as long as we were, it doesn't take much to be amused. On those interminable bus rides we thought it would be funny to make a list of the top twenty questions people asked us—sort of a Second Chapter of Acts FAQ—get them copied, and then hand them out before anyone had a chance to begin the nightly interrogation. Questions like these would have been on the list:

- "How'd you come up with the name Second Chapter?"
- "Are you guys brother and sisters?"
- "How many years have y'all been traveling?"
- "What's it like living out of a suitcase?"
- "Do you get nervous before you sing?"

We had to constantly remind ourselves that these great people had just met us and were fascinated by details that were boring to us.

So lodging in a hotel cost more, but what a wonderful change, even if the places we stayed at times were a little seedy. It didn't take long for me to grow used to sleeping in a different bed every night; I was doing that already. It was a godsend just knowing that I had a quiet room to come back to after concerts, a sanctuary in my off times.

When we had a real day off, and not just a travel day, the hotel became a place to catch up on much-needed rest. The hotel also provided me with a place where I could shower and get ready before concerts. By this time, we had a couple of tech guys who would get to the auditorium an hour or so before the rest of us to set up the equipment, so I no longer had to worry about getting my clothes dirty. Annie and Nellie still got ready in the bus just before concert. That allowed them to put on makeup and look cute and fresh before taking the stage. I was the typical guy, and it was easier for me to just show up at the hall ready to go.

A Dangerous Group

The older I get, the more I realize how true it is that you can't please everybody. Second Chapter never thought for a moment that just our name might cause someone not to attend our concerts. Because Acts 2 in the Bible gives the account of Pentecost, several denominations thought we were a cult! No, really. They were afraid of tongue talking, and some pastors would forbid members in their congregations from going to our concerts. They would say we were deceived, that we were instruments of the devil, that God couldn't use our kind of music, and so on.

For years after the group ended, people were still telling me stories that went something like this: "Our pastor told our youth group not to go to the Second Chapter concert. But we loved what you guys did—we really sensed the presence of God when you sang. So some us got together and snuck out to see you."

This fearful goofiness always upset me, and it made me conclude that Christians—at least Western Christians—are the most narrow-minded people on the planet. And that's an opinion I still pretty much hold.

When you look at history, it's plain to see that when God moved in new ways that didn't fit comfortably into the box, the new thing was automatically looked upon as the devil's work. For example, some of the precious old hymns of the church, stuffed full of doctrinal truths, borrowed their melodies from popular beer-drinking songs of the day. Back then there were those in the church who made a big stink about that, but now it's a nonissue.

When Second Chapter was rejected by different Christian groups, it hurt badly because there we were, giving our all to what we knew in our hearts God wanted us to do. And yet some of our brothers and sisters in the body of Christ said we were in league with the devil.

Some of the treatment we encountered on the road made me so appreciative of our wonderful, supportive church back home in LA. Church on the Way was an oasis for Second Chapter of Acts, and we received our spiritual grounding from Pastor Jack Hayford. Each new record we cut was prayed over by our church family before it was released. Through the years, we began to see our music ministry as an extension of Church on the Way, not in an official capacity, but simply because our ideology was so in tune with what the Lord was giving Jack. Also, because we'd grown so much in the Lord through Jack's teaching, the church just seemed a part of us. This wonderful church support base meant so much whenever we were confronted by those in the body of Christ who didn't agree with what we were doing. It helped us stay faithful to what the Lord wanted us to do.

Artists and actors were drawn to Church on the Way—people like Dean Jones, Pat Boone, Charlene Tilton, and others. The pool of musicians was so strong there that early on, Second Chapter's road band ended up consisting exclusively of players from the church. This marriage of the group and musicians from our local body was a powerful one because we were on the same page spiritually.

At our first rehearsals, I was surprised at their level of musicianship. They were much more than weekend warriors, and they were dedicated to becoming the best players possible. I had heard many grade-A studio players, which made me all the more aware of how good our band was. And they were a blast to hang out with too. We thought these guys deserved a name of their own, so we ended up being known as Second Chapter of Acts and a band called David.

A Different Drummer

As a group, we did things a little differently.

For one thing, we didn't like too much self-promotion. We didn't want to be on certain magazine covers or to be interviewed in certain ways. In short, we didn't care for hype. Sure, we wanted to inform people when we were touring so they could come if they wanted to, but we had no desire to set ourselves up as celebrities. We knew there was danger in that.

Also, we chose not to go to most of the major Christian music festivals. We much preferred ministering in auditoriums, where we could control the lighting and sound, since that made for a more intimate setting. Outdoor festivals, such as Creation, Jesus Northwest, and Go Fest, made it almost impossible to achieve any real ministry. People would be enjoying the sunshine, playing Frisbee, and smacking beach balls around, and once in a while jets would fly overhead. We were not against people having a good time; those events just were not for us. We did end up doing a few festivals through the years, since we thought maybe we were being too hard-nosed. But after every one we remembered why we had made the "no festival" decision in the first place.

During a prayer time in 1977, we sensed the Lord telling us that we should no longer depend upon ticket sales to support the ministry; we were to do offering-only concerts. Okay, Lord. This was no small step of faith considering the expense of transporting a dozen or so people and equipment from city to city. But we went for it...and God honored our decision and always took care of us.

Evolution into Ministry

The group evolved over the years, in terms of how each one of us ministered.

When we first toured, Annie did almost all the talking from the stage. I never found this odd, since most of our songs came from her experiences with the Lord. Meanwhile, Buck had become the emcee. He would come out before we did and lead the congregation in a few worship choruses. So in the early years, the two of them had stronger leadership roles, which suited me fine.

At first Nellie and I saw ourselves as "the kids," while Buck and Annie were the adults. As time passed, though, Nellie and I became young adults, and with that came change.

At the end of concerts, we never failed to give an altar call. Buck would take the stage when we had finished singing and would present the gospel. One night before we sang (I was in my early twenties by this time), Buck asked me if I would give the altar call that night. I looked at him in disbelief and said, "Why do you want me to do it?"

He said something to the effect that he felt people might respond better to the gospel if someone who had been singing all night gave the altar call.

Up to that point, I had been comfortable singing songs and letting everyone else do the convincing. I didn't think I was ready for the responsibility of leading people to Christ. Buck told me that he felt I was more than ready and said I'd had enough teaching put into me over the years to pull it off. "Present Jesus from your heart, and you won't fail," he said.

All during that concert, I tried my best to let the words Buck had spoken comfort me, but as the night wore on, I kept thinking, *There's no way I'm going to make it through this.* I was so nervous that I could hardly think straight. I was always afraid of speaking to crowds (I suppose it was nothing more than the fear of failure). When the time came for the invitation, it was all I could do to keep from gagging and begin. I stumbled through the best I could, parroting things I'd heard Buck and other pastors say. When I was finished, I was pretty surprised to see several people respond.

Buck gave me some pointers on how to do it better next time and made the decision that from then on I should do most of the altar calls.

I decided that if I was to be responsible for leading people to Christ, I would have fun doing it. It didn't take long before my personality showed up in full swing. Because I loved making people laugh, I couldn't see why altar calls should be gloomy affairs. I started out talking about evolution and how many people believe we came from a pile of goo. By the time I was ready to give the invitation, people were in tears from laughing so hard. I think for many it was the first time they had considered that a Christian could have a sense of humor.

Not long after I started stand-up-comedian altar calls, Nellie also began to use spiritual gifting that had been hidden in her. As we traveled around the country in our bus, Nellie told us that during concerts she sometimes sensed the Lord doing specific things in people while we sang. We thought it would be good for her to speak those things out loud during concert times. At first she was reluctant, but we kept encouraging her to do it.

One evening we paused between songs for Nellie to speak. I could tell she was nervous, but she found her boldness and explained to the audience that the Lord was there in the auditorium to touch people. From then on, she would say things like, "There's a man here tonight who is deaf in one ear. The Lord has touched you, and now you hear fine." Or she'd call out that someone was "touched and healed of chronic back pain." It was wild—but great!

We always encouraged people to come to one of us after the concert and confirm that the Lord had healed them. Many people indeed did come and tell us that God had worked in them the very thing Nellie had addressed. I admired her courage to step out in an area that for many years had been abused in Christian circles.

During some concerts, after Nellie called out specific healings, no one came forward and identified themselves. That was discouraging to Nellie, but she kept announcing what God was doing for people. It's gratifying to me, even now some fifteen to twenty years later, that when I do concerts, people come up to me from time to time and say, "You guys did a concert in my town years ago. Nellie said something, and the Lord touched me." I'll ask, "Did you come up and tell anyone afterward?" I'm surprised at how many say they did not. When I ask why they didn't, they give various

---

Case Closed

In 1977, Second Chapter toured with Phil Keaggy. Phil played guitar on all Second Chapter stuff, while we sang background on most of his material. The musical evening was planned so that Second Chapter would open the first half of the concert and Phil would perform the second half.

One night, after Second Chapter had finished our opening set, Phil decided to take a nap during intermission. As the break ended, though, Phil was nowhere to be found. Some of us started looking for him around the auditorium, while others looked outside. For some reason, I decided to look in our road cases, the large storage boxes we used for equipment. We had one case that was bigger than most; it was used to transport all the microphone stands. I lifted the lid, and there at the bottom was Phil fast asleep.

---

reasons. I'm always pleased to pass along their thanks to Nellie the next time I see her—she's grateful God used her in that way.

Even though the group stopped performing in 1988, I never get tired of hearing what the Lord was able to do through us. One of my absolute favorite things is to hear how someone got saved at a Second Chapter concert. Some of them have become pastors of thriving churches where I've since sung in my solo career.

While touring—and touring—all those years, we learned that the only thing we could put complete trust in was God. We couldn't trust the bus or the sound system or the lights or the number of people the sponsors told us would show up for concerts. The faithfulness of God was the one thing that never wavered.

Whenever we felt discouraged because we had performed poorly or had not met our expenses due to a small turnout, there were always people at those events who came up afterward and thanked us for the "great concert" and said how much the Lord had spoken to them. He always showed up and gave us encouragement, helping us to not focus on the good times or bad but to believe in our call and keep pressing on.

9

Road Stories

Traveling for so many years with Second Chapter of Acts, I accumulated quite a collection of stories about things that occurred to me or others in the group. Many of them are humorous; others just make a person think. All of them give the flavor of what touring was like in the 1970s and 1980s.

When You Gotta Go...

In 1977 we were doing a concert at Calvary Chapel in Costa Mesa, California. The concert was being simulcast on a Christian radio station. At one point Nellie and Annie sang "The Prince Song" that depicts the Lord as a prince who rescues a damsel. Needless to say, I didn't sing on that one. Since Annie gave a long intro, I decided to take the opportunity to visit the little boys' room.

Looking around the backstage area, I couldn't locate a bathroom. But I decided I had plenty of time to find one. I walked out the back of the building and around to the front. The church had an overflow room that seemed more accessible than going into the front of the main building. As I walked into the overflow chapel, people stared at me. Someone said, "Hey, what are you doing in here? Shouldn't you be backstage?"

I just shrugged my shoulders and said, "Gotta go."

After using the washroom in the overflow chapel, I walked back through and saw Nellie and Annie singing on the screen. I knew I didn't have much time to get back, so I quickly headed to the rear of the church and found the door I'd exited from. My heart sank as I turned the handle. The door was locked. I knew at that moment that I didn't have time to run around the church and come in the front. Nor did I want to. Sauntering down the center of a full church, with all eyes staring at me, was not something I wanted to do. So, in lieu of being totally embarrassed, I started beating on the door in hopes that someone backstage would hear me.

The moments ticked by. I knew I must be out of time by now. Finally someone let me in. As I approached the stage, I heard my sisters saying things like, "Matt, where are you?" and "Should we send someone to look for him?" As I walked onto the stage, people began clapping. I could tell my sisters were dying to know what had happened. So I walked up to the mike and without missing a beat said, "Well, when you gotta go, you gotta go."

That was a Saturday night. The next morning at our own church my embarrassment was made all the worse when my friends said, "Hey, Matt, heard you on the radio last night. Good one, Matt: 'When you gotta go, you gotta go.'"

The Halfway House

In the early years of touring, we couldn't afford to stay in hotels. Trying our best to be frugal, we would stay with host families—people who volunteered to take us in after concerts. For the most part, this arrangement worked out well. Once in a while, however, disaster struck.

One night after a concert in 1977, our guitar player Rick Azim and I found out that we would be spending the night in a halfway house—yeah, that's right—*a halfway house!* That's a place for guys who had completed their time in prison and were now getting ready for release back into society. Rick and I ended up sharing a room with one of the parolees. As we got ready to turn in for the night, the ex-con looked at us and said, "The rats haven't figured out how to climb the bedposts yet, but if they do, I can shoot them off with this." He reached under his pillow and brandished a .38 snub-nosed revolver.

Rick's face turned white as he looked my way and said, "Matt, can I talk to you for a second?"

We went upstairs and immediately called Buck. "We don't care where you put us, but it can't be here."

101 Tubas

Back in the seventies, a band member and I were introduced to the son of the family that would be hosting us that night. With introductions out of the way, we gathered our suitcases and followed the guy to his vehicle, which looked like an old cargo van. Before he opened the back doors to load our suitcases, I noticed a painting on one of the doors and asked our new friend if he was the artist.

He said yes.

I examined the painting closer and saw that it depicted two angels holding a net over what appeared to be a demon. There was a Scripture reference under the cartoon that I thought I knew. I asked the guy, "Doesn't that scripture refer to us being 'fishers of men'?"

He thought for a moment and said yes. He then went on to explain his logic behind the picture. He told us that the angels were trying to catch the demon, in an effort to get him saved.

I thought, *Do I even want to go there with this guy?* But I said something to the effect that I didn't think angels could do that kind of thing with demons.

He stared at me with a puzzled look on his face and said, "Why not?"

I told him the demons had already made their choice, and I left it at that.

After loading our suitcases, we walked around to the passenger side to get in. He opened the side cargo door, which revealed that there were no seats in the back. I thought to myself, *Well, at least one of us can ride shotgun up front.* As I opened the passenger door, though, I understood why he had opened the side door first. The only seat in the whole van was the driver's seat. The band member and I just looked at each other, shrugged our shoulders, and climbed in.

The ride to his parents' house was uncomfortable but interesting. He filled us in on what his parents liked and didn't like. At one point he told us that his dad's favorite album was *101 Tubas.* I thought the guy was pulling my leg, but when we got to his house, one of the first things he did was show me the record. *Are you kidding me?* It was all I could do not to laugh.

After meeting his parents and getting asked the top twenty questions people always seemed to ask (the apple hadn't fallen far from the tree), we bowed out of the conversation and went to our room to get ready for bed. We found out that Junior was harder to shake than a shadow. He followed us into our room and plopped himself down on one of the beds, then sat there for a half hour talking about nothing. Meanwhile, my roomie and I dropped hint after hint that we wanted him to leave so we could get some shuteye. Nothing seemed to be working; he ignored our hints and kept right on talking.

It got downright comical as we came up with more and more inventive and blatant ways to get him to go away. Finally, after nothing else worked, we had him stand up and we literally pushed him out the door and closed it behind him. Then, from the other side of the door, we heard his voice say, "Okay, then, good night." We looked at each other in disbelief and fell out laughing.

The Piano Wire of Death

This story, though interesting to recall, was never funny.

One night in 1977, while we were doing a sound check, Annie was smashing away at the piano. Nellie and I were in our usual positions, standing just off the end of the piano, when we heard a strange sound. We felt something whiz by at close range and an instant later heard it smack into the thick velvet curtain at the far side of the stage. As we turned to look, we saw what appeared to be a large wire curling its way to the stage floor.

All of this happened in a split second, and it took us a few moments to realize what had happened. The first sound we had heard was a piano string breaking. The whizzing sound was the string as it made its way across the room at lightning speed just inches from our heads. Nellie and I realized how fortunate we were. The situation became more sobering when we traced the wire's trajectory and saw that it had passed between us. If that string had hit either of us, who knows how serious the injury would have been?

The Bronco Bowl

As a group, Second Chapter was fortunate when it came to health. You might think that I would have tons of stories about our being sick on the road, but apart from the occasional cold or fever, we stayed mostly healthy.

There were, however, two times when to say we got sick would be an understatement.

The first time happened in Rockford, Illinois. We all came down with what we suspected was food poisoning. My brother-in-law Steve Greisen (Nellie's husband) was the only one who seemed immune to the bug. While everyone else was tossing their guts out, Steve kept saying things like, "I never get sick. Everyone else might get sick, but I never do. I have a cast-iron stomach." And so on. We all believed him, until a few minutes after his last remark, when he began hugging the porcelain bowl like the rest of us.

The second episode was worse by far. I recall telling the Lord that if I ever got that sick again I would just as soon be dead. We were scheduled to play the Bronco Bowl, a nightclub somewhere around Dallas, Texas. Earlier in the day, we evidently had gotten ahold of bad food, and before we reached Dallas, some of us were showing signs of food poisoning.

By the time we started setting up for the concert, most of us were "blowing and going." Somehow we managed to get through the setup, but after the sound check we were all sick in earnest. As concert time approached, we looked at one another in disbelief. How in the world could we get out there and sing? We all felt so weak, and every few minutes we were running to the bathroom.

What followed was a sad excuse for a concert. All of us, especially Buck, were of the mentality that the show must go on. We took the stage and tried to put our best foot forward, but none of us could remain onstage for more than a few minutes. As we took turns filing on- and offstage, a doctor in the audience had mercy on us and supplied us with suppositories that helped with the nausea.

Through the years I've talked with different people who attended that concert; they remember it as unorthodox but not that bad. Another miracle.

Peter and the Dog

While traveling in our shuttle bus one day, Peter York, our guitar player, was standing in the wheel well by the front door opposite the driver. Buck, who generally drove the bus, was in the middle of a conversation with Peter when Buck noticed he was getting ready to pass a pickup with the meanest-looking dog you've ever seen riding in the back.

Peter was facing the back of the bus; he had no clue we were coming up on the truck. As we started to pass, Buck asked Peter if he would stick his arm out the window. Peter had no reason to think anything was up; he thought maybe Buck wanted him to signal a vehicle. Peter obediently slid the window open and stuck his arm straight out. The timing was perfect. Buck had positioned the bus as close to the truck as he dared, just as the dog started snapping and barking, inches from Peter's fingers. I wish you could have seen the look on Peter's face as he jerked his arm back inside the bus. We all busted out laughing. Fortunately for Peter, he didn't lose any digits.

European Food Wars

Every few years we would do a European tour. For some reason, we seemed to pull more pranks on one another while overseas than when traveling in the States. Maybe you could chalk it up to jet lag, or maybe it was because we traveled in two separate vans. I don't know. Anyway, certain band members would gravitate to one van over the other, so we would end up with pretty much the same people riding in the same vans every day. I thought that was great, because I knew which van to sabotage.

On one of these tours, we had been in Europe for some time when those of us in my van noticed a peculiar aroma coming from somewhere inside. For a long time we tried and failed to figure out what the smell was and where it was coming from. We finally located the source of the stench: a big ball of cheese that someone from the other van had strategically placed under one of our seats, where it would stew in the summer heat. Everyone in the other van got a big laugh when we busted them over it.

A few days later, we had some fruit—a banana and some other squishy fruit chunks—that we let get funky. I think there may have been a ham sandwich thrown in the mix as well. We were somewhere in Germany or France where it was hilly, and we had gained some distance on the other van. As we began to crest one of the hills, I talked the driver into stopping our van on the other side. After he had pulled off the road, a few of us jumped out and ran partway back up the hill. Then we hid in a trench beside the roadway and waited.

Finally we saw the top of the other van popping over the hill. That was our cue. We scrambled out of the ditch with our overripe bombs in hand. The other van had no time to react as we unleashed the fury of the weapons of goo. Our aim was true. The mushy concoction splattered into the center of their windshield and covered a large area. Vengeance was sweet.

Fresh Milk at a Price

In 1980, when Second Chapter was touring Australia and New Zealand, Kirk Herring—Buck's son from a previous marriage—was traveling with us to help with setting up and tearing down equipment. Kirk ended up rooming with me in a New Zealand hotel. On the second night we were there, I asked Kirk if he would jump up and grab me a milk carton out of the refrigerator located halfway down the corridor.

We had both turned in for the night, so he was in his birthday suit. He said, "I don't have any clothes on, and I'm too tired to put any on."

I said, "Just run down the hallway and grab me a milk. It's late; no one will see you."

"There's no way I'm going to run down that hallway buck naked," he said, "because I know as soon as I get out there, you'll slam the door behind me."

"No way, man. I'm tired. Just go out there and get me some milk."

After we went back and forth for some time about my not closing him out, I convinced him that I was too tired to mess around with that sort of game. He finally decided to take the chance. So, dressed in nothing but his skin, out the door he scurried. As soon as he rounded the corner for the refrigerator, I jumped out of bed and slammed the door behind him.

He ran back, infuriated. He banged loudly on the door, yelling for me to let him in the room. He was only loud for a second, though, because he quickly realized that Buck and Annie's room was directly across from ours. So his next knock on the door was so quiet that you could barely hear it, and it was followed by the funniest sound I had ever heard. He was saying in a whisper, "Matt, let me in. Man, this isn't funny. Come on, man, let me in."

I waited for what must have seemed an eternity to Kirk before I opened that door. He was so upset that he was shaking. I just couldn't help myself—I had to do it. The best part was that he still had the milk in his hands, which of course I took and drank.

Mystery Food in Dijon and the Wrinkled Men

It was lunchtime as we pulled into Dijon, France, in 1980. All of us were hungry, and we located what looked to be an adequate little café. Once we were all seated, the waiter came to our tables with menus. The menus didn't have a word of English on them, and no one in our group spoke a word of French.

After finding out there were no menus in English and that no one in the restaurant spoke our language, we began the hilarious task of trying to decide what food the menu described. We all ordered items according to what seemed like something we might eat. There was no science to this. Some band members ordered things simply because they liked the sound of the words describing the different food items.

As the orders began showing up, most people had good luck with their

Snowing in the Bus

After a while, when you've been on the road for, say, six weeks straight, you can develop what I call the "What day is it?" syndrome. It was hard for me not to be completely bored on the bus. I had to invent entertainment.

One winter day I noticed that snow was slowly sifting in through the air-conditioning vent over the back row of the bus. With no one paying attention, I went to the rear of the bus, brushed off the snow that had accumulated on the seat, sat down, and let the snow pile up on top of my head. I waited quite a while, until a good layer of snow was covering my head and shoulders. When I felt my personal snow drift had reached a comical enough level, I began singing "Our God Snows" to the tune of "Our God Reigns."

It got a good laugh.

food choices. When mine came, however, it looked nothing like what I had pictured. In my mind, I'd ordered a steak smothered in a wonderful sauce, with a side of glazed vegetables and french fries. In reality, my lunch was a bowl of weak broth with some kind of bone in the middle. The bone had hardly any meat on it, and the broth was the most unexciting excuse for soup I'd ever seen.

I'm an adventurous eater—I'll eat almost anything. But the meal was so far removed from anything I had anticipated that it was beyond disappointing. I pictured the chef in the kitchen saying to the waiter, "These Americans don't speak a word of French. We can give them anything and they won't know the difference. Let's give the guy with the long blond hair this leftover bone junk; he'll probably eat it and love it."

Sitting at a table near us were two ancient Frenchmen whose faces were so wrinkled that they looked more like Shar-Pei dogs than humans. Our drummer Mike Celenza was sitting next to Nellie. As the meal progressed, one of the wrinkled-up French guys kept giving Mike the wink and the nod toward Nellie, as if to say, "Ooh-la-la, sonny boy, why aren't you making your move on this lovely young woman?"

That lunch experience was one we laughed over for years.

Lost in Zurich

One night, after a concert in Zurich, Switzerland, we piled into the van to head back to our hotel. We ended up getting so utterly lost that it became comical. Everybody had a different idea as to what direction we should be heading in, but our driver—guitar player Curt Bartlett—insisted he could get us back.

After we drove around for the better part of an hour, we found ourselves in some sort of industrial park in the middle of nowhere. Curt, being completely at a loss, suggested we all take turns calling out the direction in which we thought we should go, figuring it couldn't get any worse. It became a game. One of us would yell out, "Turn right," and we would go that way for a while. Then someone else would yell, "Turn left." We did this for some time. We started laughing so hard that we didn't even care how lost we were.

What amazes me is that—as insane as this sounds—our direction-by-committee approach actually worked. We eventually pulled into the parking lot of the hotel.

Blinded by the Light

During one Second Chapter tour, we started our concerts by playing a tape with an instrumental song on it. As the song was playing, we would take our places on the stage. The stage was totally dark until the song ended, at which time the lights would come up and we would go straight into our first number.

Normally, this wasn't a problem, because the stages were easily accessible. But then one night we were getting ready for a concert at a large Florida church that didn't have a backstage area. Instead, they had a choir room at the top of some stairs above the stage.

As the music was reaching the point where we needed to get ourselves into position, we made the mistake of not turning off the lights in the choir room to give our eyes time to grow accustomed to the dark stage below. We switched off the lights and opened the door to the sanctuary, only to realize that we could see *nothing*. We ended up crawling feet first down the steps leading to the stage.

Unlike us, the audience had been sitting in the dark for some time.

Though we couldn't see a thing, they could see us as plain as day. They began to snicker and then laugh out loud as members of the "famed" Second Chapter of Acts stumbled into things on their way down to the stage.

Jim Tenneboe, our keyboard player, became aware of our predicament and tried to help us by shining his flashlight so we could see. The only problem with this was that the beam of the flashlight was shone directly into our eyes—no help there.

We finally made it—but that wasn't quite the effect we'd been looking for to open our concert.

Suicide Deer

To this day, it's one of the weirdest things I've ever seen.

I was sitting in the back of our tour bus, as we were rolling from one town to another, when I noticed a deer several hundred yards away in an open field. The deer was running parallel to our bus. As we gained on the deer, I noticed it was now running at an angle toward us. I saw there was a fence between us, so I figured the deer would run along the fence until we passed.

Now, that deer could have gone any number of ways; nothing was restricting its choice of direction. Yet to my surprise, as we drew closer, the deer kept heading at full speed toward the fence and our bus. When it got to the fence, it didn't miss a step and leaped over the barrier. There we were, zooming down the freeway at seventy miles an hour, and with perfect timing, the deer intersected our path and slammed into the side of the bus. Freaked me out. It was like the deer had put a lot of thought into getting the timing just right and decided that a collision with this bus was as good a way to go as any.

Born to Run

One night, after a concert in the mid-1980s, Second Chapter was committed to take part in a fund-raiser telethon for a local television station. By the time we arrived at the station, we were already exhausted. I recall thinking, *What in the world have we gotten ourselves into?* We decided to have mercy on our band guys, so we just had Jim Tenneboe, our keyboard player, accompany us.

Everyone at the station proved to be more than nice to us. The host of the program had the typical television-evangelist haircut, all puffed up and sprayed. (As Sting puts it, "They all look like game show hosts to me.") We were also introduced to a young guy who worked as the floor director. He proved to be one of the most hyperactive, animated humans I've ever met. The show was live, so we were at one end of the studio, with the host at the other end. As we sang our first song, "hyper boy" ran around behind the cameras, getting our attention by frantically waving his arms and pointing to the camera that would go live next. Of course, it's not like we hadn't done television before. The red light glowing on top was a pretty good indicator as to which camera was on. The floor director's mannerisms were so over the top that it was all we could do to keep straight faces.

When our song was finished, they cut to the host, who talked for a few minutes. With about a minute left before we were to go live with another song, "hyper boy" came running up to me and asked if we were ready. I gave him the thumbs-up, and for some reason I said to him, "Born to run." The kid gave me a knowing look and darted off toward the host.

Seconds before we were to sing, I saw the kid lean over and say something in the host's ear. The host then looked into the camera and said, "Let's welcome back Second Chapter of Acts as they perform their new song called 'Born to Run.'"

That totally did me in. Jim started playing the intro to our song, but he was laughing under his breath so hard that you could see his shoulders shaking. Nellie and I were busting up with laughter. It only got worse with the thought of being on live television.

As Jim shook his way through the intro, it came time to begin singing. That particular song was supposed to start with all three of us, but for the whole first verse, Nellie and I were laughing so hard that all we could do was mouth the words and let Annie take it. The technicians in the sound booth must have thought something was wrong with their equipment, as we looked like we were singing, but nothing could be heard from the two of us. Jim, Nellie, and I finally pulled it together enough to finish the song.

Oh Boy, Perth Amboy

I've seen some unusual things while traveling around to perform concerts, but this next story ranks among the weirdest.

One night, after a Second Chapter concert in Perth Amboy, New Jersey, my sisters and I did what we always did—we stayed after to minister to people, praying for needs and so on. After a while, I could see that the ministry time was winding down, so I went to the back of the auditorium to talk with some people. All of a sudden, I noticed a commotion near the stage area. Some of our band guys, along with a few local people, were praying for a woman who was "manifesting" by making strange growling noises. I don't like to miss out on the action, so I quickly made my way back to the front of the auditorium. By the time I got there, this woman was in full swing.

The auditorium had foldable chairs, and this lady had single-handedly (well, with the help of her "visitors") sent four rows of chairs in different directions. It took five men to restrain her. She was growling and speaking in a man's voice, yelling out commands and obscenities. Foam began to drip from her mouth. It shocked me. It's not that I didn't believe someone could be possessed (over the years I'd seen plenty of people who were), I'd just never seen anyone act like this.

After a few minutes of people's praying for this woman and commanding the demons to leave in the name of Jesus, the woman's appearance changed markedly. She quit foaming, growling, and yelling like a man and became very still. Moments later she sat up, and someone offered her a drink of water. She just looked at him and said in a meek feminine voice, "No thanks, I've just had a drink of living water."

10

The Lindale Years

The Hollywood mansion, since it was a rental, served as our home only for a couple of years after Nellie and I moved in with Buck and Annie.

After that, Second Chapter called a number of areas in California home while we were between tours. We lived in several places in the Los Angeles area, as well as in Burbank, Wilmington, and Northridge. For a while, we even lived in the tiny community of Rio Nido, on the Russian River north of San Francisco.

My favorite—and the place we stayed the longest—was the house in Northridge. I loved that it had a swimming pool and fruit trees. Buck even built a music studio there. When it came time to leave, Buck was concerned about whether he'd be able to sell the place, because how many people want a music studio in their house? But as it turned out, that studio worked to our favor when Jeffrey Osborne, the soul singer, bought the house.

All of us were Californians. We had no plans to ever leave our home state, but by 1980, to our surprise, a friend had convinced us to move to the little town of Lindale in East Texas.

Keith

A few years before we moved to Texas, I met a musician by the name of Keith Green. At first I didn't know what to make of him. He was so hyperactive (the pot calling the kettle black?) that in many ways he took the cake for being the "strange musician" type. I don't recall exactly how we met, but it wasn't long before I was driving over to Keith's house and listening to him sing while he assaulted his poor piano. (Keith broke piano strings because he played so hard. I saw him do it more than once.) One time I spent the night at his place after a not-so-successful day of writing music together. Keith was a major night owl; he'd go to bed late and wake up late, which suited me fine.

After Keith and I got to know each other, we did some unusual work together. The two of us, and a studio guitar player named Mike Deasy, began recording background vocals for an older woman who had more money than talent. Her husband was the president of a large corporation, and to appease his wife, he had built her a recording studio upstairs in their Bel Air mansion. This studio, which rivaled any I had seen in Los Angeles, had a forty-track tape machine, a large recording console, and even television cameras. The husband would hire Keith, Mike, and me to sing on programs he'd produce so his wife could be on television. Once the shows were finished, they would purchase airtime on UHF channels.

Working with Keith and Mike was a blast, and it was easy money. Most of the songs were classics, which I enjoyed singing. One day we were working on a song, and Mike just couldn't get his part right. Keith and I kept ribbing him about messing up until it got to the point where Keith and I were actually rolling on the ground with laughter. Mike didn't find it at all funny. Finally, he got so upset that he hauled off and kicked me so hard in the butt (he had on pointy cowboy boots) that I thought I was going to pass out.

The corporation head treated us nicely. He'd come into the control room every now and then to see how things were going, but for the most part he let us do our thing. He had his chef make us lunch every day. One time he served steak, which we ate in the studio around a table complete with silverware (and I mean silver), linen tablecloth, crystal, and disposable paper napkins that were stamped with the initials of the executive and his wife in twenty-four-carat gold leaf. I almost felt guilty wiping my hands and mouth with them.

Keith started making albums of his own music with a producer named Bill Maxwell. Bill, who had played drums with Andraé Crouch, went on to produce all of Keith's music through the years. On one of Keith's early recordings, Bill thought it might be good to hire me to do some background vocals. I showed up for the session and began working on vocal ideas for different songs.

As the session progressed, Bill decided he wanted me to try some of my trademark vocal gymnastics on one of the cuts. As I honed in on what Bill was after, I could tell by Keith's facial expressions that he wasn't thrilled with what I was doing. Even though I couldn't hear what was being said because of a thick piece of glass separating us, the emotions were almost palpable.

Finally Keith couldn't stand it any longer. His objections grew so loud that I could hear him in spite of the glass. He was yelling things like, "I don't want that kind of crap on my record." This put a halt to the session. (Some years later, though, Keith and I worked together on his project called *So You Wanna Go Back to Egypt*. That experience was a lot more pleasant. We recorded in Brown Bannister's studio, located in his house in the San Fernando Valley.)

At this time, Keith was still a new Christian. I'd never met anyone with as much reckless zeal for the Lord. I always thought of him as a bull in a china shop. Keith had a way of challenging everything and everybody. He was truly an evangelist at heart. At one of his early concerts, he gave a most unusual altar call. He'd have everyone stand up, ask the Christians to sit down, then ask those who were left standing why they were standing. He was a kind of a modern-day John the Baptist.

One day Keith asked if I would be his prayer partner. At first I thought he was joking, but I learned early on that Keith hardly every joked about such matters. He explained to me that he was facing some things he wasn't comfortable sharing with his followers. (Keith's Last Days Ministries grew quickly from a few people living at his house to several houses full of people.) We got together a couple of times for prayer, but I had always looked upon Keith as just a friend. It seemed strange that he would share important ministry things with me, and I felt uncomfortable.

In many ways Keith and I were like oil and water. I loved him dearly, but I found that I couldn't hang out with him for long periods of time. I'm more of a water-off-a-duck's-back kind of guy, but Keith always seemed to have this pit-bull intensity no mater what topic he was sinking his teeth into. Most of the time Keith acted as if he knew his time on earth was short, and he wanted to make the most of it for the kingdom.

It wasn't long before Keith recognized that he was going to have to make different living arrangements for his ministry, which in those days was more of a commune than anything else. He quickly outgrew the houses his ministry was headquartered in around the Los Angeles area, and he decided to look for other possibilities. He ended up finding some land in Texas, and Second Chapter financially helped him make the move.

After Keith had been in Texas for a few months, he called and told us about a hundred-acre parcel of land for sale adjacent to his property. Second Chapter had been considering a move as well. There was a ten-acre plot of land in Los Angeles that we were getting close to purchasing, but when we heard about this land in Texas and realized we could buy one hundred acres for less than the ten would cost in Southern California, we began to seriously consider it. Buck went to Texas to look at the land and then gave us a report.

We talked through all the pros and cons of moving to Texas. The pros: land was cheaper; Texas had no state income tax; we would be centrally located for touring; the cost of living was considerably less; and so on. For

O Christmas Tree

Not long after Second Chapter moved to Texas, Keith Green came by our temporary house to talk to Buck. It was Christmastime, and Keith was going through a kick where he thought it was wrong to have a Christmas tree in the home. He banned them from his ministry, because he said the practice was based on some kind of pagan ritual that dated back five hundred years. We disagreed with his argument and celebrated Christmas with all the trappings, including the tree.

As I saw Keith pull into our driveway, I waited for him to come into the house. The only way to get to the area where he would meet with Buck was to come right by our Christmas tree. As I heard him entering, I knelt at the base of the tree and acted as if I were worshiping it. I said things like, "O mighty Christmas tree, your branches are so beautiful."

As Keith walked behind me, his only response was to say, "Jerk."

I had a good laugh—and Keith allowed Christmas trees after that.

me the cons hinged more on personal preferences than anything else. For starters, I would have to move away from all the friends I'd made over the last ten years. I would miss the ocean. (I loved the beach. My favorite pastime in the summer was body surfing.) And the weather in East Texas, from what I could gather, left a lot to be desired. I certainly was less than enthusiastic about moving, but in the end I saw the value and decided to sign on.

After we bought the property, Annie designed a building that would eventually have three apartments, a large area for our bus and truck, a recording studio, and a full-size tournament-designed racquetball court. Buck, Annie, and I had grown to love racquetball while we lived in Los Angeles.

After the new building was finished, when we weren't on the road, I normally played racquetball for an hour or so a day, except on Sundays.

During the summer of 1982, David Wilkerson invited Second Chapter of Acts to go with him to New York City for some inner-city ministry. On about our fourth day in New York, after we had come back to our hotel following the day's ministry, someone knocked on my door. Buck was standing there with an unusual look on his face. I asked him what was up, and he told me something that seemed surreal. He had just gotten off the phone with some folks at Last Days Ministries. Keith had died in a plane crash off the end of their runway in East Texas. Details were sketchy, but Buck understood that there were no survivors.

For the next few days—and indeed long after we got back home—I functioned in a haze of disbelief.

Shortly after returning from New York, I took a walk to locate the crash site. This wasn't morbid curiosity; I was looking for some kind of closure. I walked to the end of the Last Days Ministries runway, climbed a barbed-wire fence, and headed in the direction that I believed would take me to the site.

As I walked, I saw a line of trees with their tops broken off. Once I located the crash site, I realized that it was less than a mile from where I lived.

The plane wreckage had only recently been hauled off by the FAA, and as I walked around the scorched site, I found little pieces of debris. One of the objects was a light from one of the wings. The glass was cracked but still in place. I still have that light—it sits on one of my speakers in my music room. I've kept it to remember Keith and as a reminder of how fragile life is, so that I won't take it for granted.

Keith is greatly missed, not just by his family and by countless fans, but by me, his friend. His death left a void in the body of Christ.

Wally

When we moved to Texas, my brother Jack moved along with us and became a permanent part of what Second Chapter was doing. A friend of ours, Wally Duguid, also came along.

I was about fourteen when I met Wally. He showed up one day at our door in Hollywood, dressed like a hippie with long hair and bare feet. (Wally was kicked out of our church once because he refused to wear shoes.) We soon found out that Wally had a knack for electronics, and he actually built our first sound board. He was a part of our lives for many years, and though he didn't live with us, he was always there when we needed his help.

Wally never ceased to amaze me; he was always tinkering with some kind of gadget. One time I went to his house (this was while we still lived in Los Angeles), and he took me out to his garage to show me a car he was working on. The car was some sort of hybrid with batteries to supplement the gas-powered engine. I don't think he ever perfected it, but when you realize the year was 1975, you understand how clever and ahead of his time he was.

When Wally moved to Texas with us, he had already been married for some years. He and his wife, Marianne, started building a house about three miles from our building. Wally asked if Jack and I would help him with some of the interior construction. Never one who did anything conventionally, Wally had ordered a house with a prefabricated shell. It was left up to the owner to finish the inside. Jack and I were getting cramped, living in our temporary house, so we asked Wally if we could stay in his house while we helped finish it.

I don't think that in the history of modern home building there has been a house better insulated than this one. Once fiberglass insulation was placed between the studs, Wally had Jack and me staple a plastic shield over any area that was to receive drywall or Sheetrock. Once the plastic was in place, we began the Sheetrock work. Hanging wallboard is difficult enough, but remember, this was Wally's house. We started off with half-inch Sheetrock, and when we were done with that, we went back over the first layer with another layer of even thicker Sheetrock. By the time we got done with the ceilings, my back was thrashed.

I doubt Wally and Marianne ever feel a draft inside the superinsulated walls of their Texas fortress.

Jack

By the time Jack and I finished work on Wally's house, we had grown stir-crazy. Second Chapter didn't normally tour in the winter months, so Jack and I thought, *Why should we hang around here freezing? Let's go do something.*

In recent years, Jack had discovered snow skiing. I had never had much of a desire to ski, since all my friends seemed to come back from ski trips with broken legs. But Jack kept trying to convince me that if I tried skiing, I'd love it. So, after much discussion, we came up with the idea of taking a road trip and hitting ski resorts all over the West. We both were single and had few responsibilities. Why not?

At the time, both of us had plenty of cash, but neither of us wanted to spend it on housing. So I called a few friends to line up free lodging. Before we knew it, we were out the door, heading for California in Jack's 1968 fastback Mustang for a two-month ski trip.

The first stop was Los Angeles, where I bought my skis and boots. The second stop was Mammoth Mountain, a ski resort near Yosemite. Before the move to Texas, I had met a girl at church who'd told me that anytime I wanted to ski Mammoth I should stay with her parents, who lived there. I gave her a call, and she lined up everything with her folks.

Jack and I drove into the mountains. We found the cabin and were greeted by my friend's parents. For some reason, they were expecting four girls in their late teens; instead, they got two guys in their early twenties. I saw the look of confusion cross their faces. But rather than telling Jack and me to take a hike, they warmly welcomed us into their home.

It was the perfect skiing arrangement. Our lodging was free. We'd get up in the morning, put on our ski clothing, grab our equipment, catch a shuttle bus half a block from the house, get dropped off at the ski lifts, and ski all day.

Just about every day we were the first ones in line to go up the mountain and the last ones to ski off the mountain. Most people stopped for lunch, but not Jack and me. We figured the lift tickets were expensive, and the old Ward mentality of squeezing every drop of fun out of something kicked in.

I did things on skis that I wouldn't dream of doing today. The fun for me was not all the technical stuff you have to learn to be a better skier but in seeing how far I could travel through the air or how high I could get or how many runs I could make in a single day. We'd launch ourselves off tree stumps or fly off any sort of snow mound we could find. By the time we arrived back on the last shuttle of the day, we were beat. My legs were shot, the muscles twitching and shaking.

When we left Mammoth, we drove up north to visit the rest of our brothers in the Sacramento area. But we stayed there for only a few days—we were on a mission. After leaving Sacramento, we headed east and stopped off at Heavenly Valley for more skiing.

We had a friend named Jerry who lived in the Heavenly Valley area. Jerry had done some concert booking for Second Chapter and was kind enough to line up a place for us to stay. Our hosts had a log house where they held prayer meetings once a week. Because Jack and I hung around for over a week, we attended the meeting.

When one of the attendees started to pray, I noticed that the gentleman had a speech impediment. He kept saying the phrase "Lord Jesus," but it came out sounding like "laud de buss." And as he continued, he asked "God the Father" to do this or that, but it came out sounding like "gut da fudda." It got to the point where Jack and I couldn't keep a straight face any longer. We actually ended up chuckling out loud, with everyone looking at us. Once the meeting concluded, we tried to explain ourselves to our host. He wasn't especially understanding, and I don't blame him.

After two more skiing stops, at Snowbird in Utah and Monarch in Colorado, we packed up our gear and headed for Texas. Not long after our return from the ski trip, Jack and I once again found ourselves bored. One day we noticed two horses in a field behind our house. As we approached the fence, both animals came over to see what we were up to. Rubbing the horses' manes and talking to them, we got the hare-brained idea to climb up on the fence and jump on the backs of these horses. I had not ridden horses that much, and riding bareback was completely new to me, but I was ready to give it a try.

When we hopped off the fence and onto the horses, they took off like a shot. Jack's steed went one way; mine another. We had no idea what we were doing, so we just hung on for dear life. Jack managed to gain a modicum of control over his ride, but the tighter I hung on to my horse, the faster it ran. Both Jack and I were scared to death, but as we'd pass each other in the field, we'd let out a tribal yell.

After a few minutes, my horse decided it didn't want me riding any longer. The horse used different methods to try to shake me off. First it headed for low-hanging tree branches. When that didn't work, it headed straight for the barbed-wire fence and at the last second turned on a dime, trying to send me flying. I hung on. Finally I waited for the horse to make one of its turning maneuvers, and as it slowed, I jumped off. Jack successfully bailed off his horse as well.

Jack and I got a big laugh out of that experience. But the owner of the horses, when he found out about what we'd done, wasn't so amused. He came over and gave us a piece of his mind.

After we apologized for riding without permission, the horses' owner settled down and we got to talking. He told us that he normally rode those horses bareback too.

"How do you control that horse without a bridle?" I asked. "The tighter I hung onto its mane, the faster he went."

The owner just looked at me and started laughing.

"What's so funny?"

"The way you make a horse run faster is to grab its mane tighter."

Oh.

Country Boy

Before the move to Texas, even with all my early exploits outdoors in North Dakota and along the American River in Sacramento, I was pretty much a city—California—boy.

For example, I had little interest in guns or fishing. It wasn't long after settling in Texas, however, that I got into collecting firearms and learned how to fish. In LA it would have been hard to find areas where I could fire a gun. As far as fishing went, it had just never appealed to me. Now we had a hundred acres of land to shoot on, and I met people who showed me the joys of fishing.

My first weapon was a .22 rifle. The beauty of a .22 is that you can buy a box of shells for next to nothing. I fired that gun a lot. And the more I began to enjoy shooting, the more I wanted to try other caliber guns.

Canton, Texas, about thirty miles from where I lived, had a swap meet called First Mondays. This fair offered everything from livestock to antiques, but the thing that interested me the most was guns. I purchased my first handgun at that fair, with absolutely no paperwork to be filled out. (That's the way they did it then.)

After I had acquired a few handguns (most of them small caliber), I bought my first twelve-gauge shotgun. If you lived in Texas, you had to have a twelve gauge. Everybody had a twelve gauge. The first time I fired that shotgun, I was surprised at how hard it kicked and how destructive it was. I would aim the shotgun barrel at a large breadfruit tree we had growing on the property, pull the trigger, and—*poof*—the breadfruit would disappear.

Now, as for fishing, years earlier, an oil company had built a five-acre pond on our property so they would have water for their machinery. They called these types of ponds tanks. I was surprised to find out that our tank had a good number of fish in it. Over the years, I caught quite a few large-mouth bass there.

Besides wetting a line in the tank, I often used it as a shooting range. I'd take all kinds of stuff down to the pond: bottles, cans, old electronic gear—just about anything that would sink if you busted it or filled it with enough holes. My favorite targets were bottles. There was something strangely satisfying about shooting the tops off bottles and sending them to the bottom. If someone ever drains that lake, they'll be amazed at the strange items on the bottom.

After I got used to the twelve gauge, I moved on to bigger and better things. My next purchases were larger caliber handguns. Eventually I bought the largest handgun I could find, a .44 Magnum Smith and Wesson model 29. The thing I loved about this gun was that I didn't have to hit a target dead on to get the devastating results I wanted.

East Texas summers were just too hot, so the best times of the year to get outdoors were the first few weeks of spring and fall. During those times I would often take long walks on our property, toting along one or more guns. Between our land and that owned by Last Days, I had a total of nearly six hundred acres to run around on. One of my favorite places to shoot was a dump site located in a remote area on Last Days property. Whenever the folks at Last Days renovated a building, they hauled many replaced items to this site. Over the years, that gave me some interesting objects to shoot up. (I guess it's no longer a secret who shot the heck out of their stuff.)

When I'd take walks in the fall, many times deer would seem to appear from nowhere. I was always surprised that you wouldn't see them until you were right on top of them. One year Chris Snell and I were walking on Last Days land. We both had just finished blasting a bunch of breadfruit off the trees with our twelve gauges, and we still had our earplugs in, so we were speaking loudly. Seconds later we came to a clearing where there were seven good-sized deer. As we came closer, the deer finally ambled off. Our blasting and yelling seemingly hadn't disturbed them at all.

It took a while, but this California boy adapted to Texas the best he could and became a country boy. I grew to love the hilly landscape, with its pines and oak trees and scattering of lakes. For the record, like a good Texan, I drove a pickup truck—without a gun rack. The weather and isolation took its toll, but the Lone Star state was good to me. We stayed there until our family moved to Colorado in 1998.

While in Texas, I finished my time with Second Chapter of Acts, started my solo singing career, met and married my wife, fathered my three girls, and faced the biggest physical challenge of my life—a lot of living during the Lindale years.

11

Perfect Union

Like much else in my life, my songwriting technique has been a bit off the wall.

In my earlier days of doing my own recording, when it came time to record a new song, I'd come up with a melodic idea first and then formulate it into what I thought would become verses, choruses, and a bridge. I'd guess at how many verses and choruses I might want and then try to figure out how the song might end. Next, I would hire musicians to come into the studio and put their parts down. When the majority of the tracks were finished, I'd start fitting lyrics into those structures.

Needless to say, that could be a hard thing to do, and at times it became nearly impossible—I had musically painted myself into a corner. I'd take rough mixes of the unfinished tracks home on cassette and play them over and over until something in the track would inspire me to write about a certain topic. Once I had the idea in my head of what the song was going to be about, it often didn't take me long to hammer out the lyrics.

It was during one of these songwriting days that I formulated the concept for the song "Perfect Union." After spending some hours listening to my cassette, going over and over the track, I finally got the lyrics finished.

"Perfect Union" was about marriage from a Christian perspective. As I usually did when I finished a song, I grabbed my wife, Deanne, sat her down, and sang the new song for her. I wanted her opinion. When I finished this one, she was crying. At first, I thought, *Hey, it wasn't that bad.* But then I realized she was touched by what she'd heard. She looked at me with tears in her eyes and said, "You wrote a song for me."

Instead of saying yes, like anybody with sense would have done, I told her the song wasn't specifically about us but marriage in general. I could tell she was disappointed, so I explained further that the song couldn't be about us since one of the verses talked about troubled times in marriage—and we hadn't had any bad times! It was a good save, but I knew I was going to have to write her a love song eventually.

I redeemed myself a few years later when I wrote "Since I Found You," a love song specifically for Deanne.

God blessed me with a wonderful wife, who is just the right fit for me. It was a long road getting there, though.

Girls

As a young boy, still living at home in Sacramento not long after my mother had died, I listened to my brothers tell stories of their dating experiences. My brother Frank's stories were by far the most colorful. He would spin tales of what he had done with his girlfriends, leaving out none of the graphic (actually, pornographic) details. He either didn't notice my presence during these tale-telling sessions or didn't care that I was pretty young to be hearing such things.

On the wall of the garage at our house, next to the washer and dryer, hundreds of phone numbers were written in pencil. Most of these phone numbers had girls' names next to them. I found out one day that the majority of these numbers belonged to girls Frank had dated.

One day I got the courage to ask him if he'd had sex with all those girls. Frank looked down at me with a smug expression and said yes.

Images and ideas were placed in my tender mind during those days that should never have been put there. I didn't identify it as such for many years, but there was a lot of deep spiritual warfare going on in my troubled heart.

My mom had died (had left me, as it appeared to me), and that hurt deeply. And I never wanted to hurt like that again. After the death of my father, too, I came up with a mechanism for dealing with potential pain: I never let anyone, especially girls, get close enough to hurt me. That's not to say I didn't have friends; I just developed the ability to maneuver and twist through the thicker fabrics of relationships without getting tangled in them. As long as I could make people laugh and have a fun time, that was good enough.

As I got older and became interested in the fairer sex, I developed a more sophisticated immune system. For the most part, I didn't respect girls, emotionally or physically. They became more like objects of challenge—things to conquer. This allowed me to keep my heart from being vulnerable.

Those years were troubling because, on the one hand, I really liked people. But on the other hand, I couldn't find the courage to let them in. Mixed into the equation was the inner fight I was having with my faith. How could I justify my behavioral patterns with people and call myself a Christian?

At the time I didn't feel there was anyone I could talk to about the issues I was trying to work out. I had a sister as a mother figure and, as I saw it, a heavy-handed brother-in-law as a father figure. I was afraid of being honest with Buck. Because his upbringing was so different from mine, I didn't think he could relate to what I was going through. My fear of saying the wrong thing around him outweighed my desire to take the chance. I ended up saying nothing at all.

I had a few girlfriends over the years, but most of those relationships were short-lived. Some relationships were with girls I had met on the road, but it was hard to maintain long-distance relationships. I didn't know how to act, and though I managed for the most part to stay out of serious trouble, I knew I couldn't handle the responsibility of trying to stay clean. I knew I didn't have what it took to continue saying no to my flesh, so the only way I could see for me to stay out of trouble was not to date at all.

It was hard to avoid one situation I encountered during those early years of Second Chapter touring. As I said earlier, we did not stay in hotels but spent our nights with people who opened their homes to us.

Sometimes I ended up with people who had a girl about my age. It normally wasn't much of a problem—unless the daughters belonged to pastors. I'm not sure why, but the stories I'd heard about PKs (pastors' kids) being wild seemed true. More times than not, the PKs proved to be the most rebellious, most out-of-control kids. As a young teenager, I had a hard time because many of these girls were pretty and more than willing to do things with me that I knew I just couldn't do. Fortunately, for the most part I was able to resist the devil, so to speak, but I certainly made out with some of them.

For several years, one woman brought her teenage daughter to our concerts when we came through their town. The mom had it in her head that her girl was the one for me. This lady would present her daughter to me after concerts, then she'd disappear into the shadows while we conversed. No question, the girl was beautiful, but it was uncomfortable to have her mom trying to set us up. Plus, the girl was a bit young for me.

After about the third time this happened, after I'd finished an evening of singing to the Lord, the girl pulled me aside and handed me a Polaroid. The picture was of her climbing into her bunk bed wearing nothing but a skimpy piece of lingerie. I really didn't need to see that, and I have no idea whether her mom knew about it or not. But I wasn't about to run the risk of showing it to her mom and have her say, "Isn't that a lovely picture?" I took the photo, stuck it in my pocket, and threw it in the trash at my earliest convenience. As it turned out, that was the last time I saw either of them. Whew.

Another time, after a concert a girl came up and asked if she could talk to me in private.

I thought, *She must want me to pray with her about something she's uncomfortable saying in front of others.* So I said, "Sure."

After we rounded a corner, she said, "Would you sign these for me?" As she exposed her breasts, my mouth dropped open. I instantly came up with a new policy that I've stuck with ever since. "I don't sign flesh," I told her.

She seemed disappointed and walked off.

If it wasn't so sad, I could have found it comical. I thought the devil was going to have to be a little more subtle than that. To this day, I chuckle when little kids come up to me, asking me to sign their hand or arm, and I tell them, "I'm sorry. I don't sign flesh."

Developing Feelings

Three years after Second Chapter moved to Texas, when I was twenty-three, the Chicago-based group Resurrection Band booked a concert in Tyler. Since they wanted to just bring their instruments, they asked Second Chapter if they could borrow our PA system and lights. We had known the guys for years, and so we said yes. The only proviso we put on the agreement was that Wally Duguid and I would have to be there to oversee everything and make sure they didn't blow up our equipment.

The night of the event, I was sitting in the auditorium, waiting for the concert to start, when I noticed a group of college-age girls looking for seats. One of them caught my attention. She had incredibly deep, beautiful blue eyes, framed by a gorgeous head of thick, dark hair.

I did all I could to get this girl to sit next to me, but I could tell she was having no part of it. (She told me later that the reason she didn't want to sit by me was simply because she didn't know me.) So instead I positioned myself directly behind her. I proceeded to roll up my program and use it as a megaphone, saying anything that came to mind that I thought she might find amusing. I guess I didn't drive her too batty, because after the concert, we ended up speaking to one another for a while.

Her name was Deanne Paul, and she was eighteen. She was from Rockford, Illinois, and her family was relatively conservative and deeply devout, highly involved in their Assembly of God church back home. Deanne was living at Twin Oaks Ranch—a Youth With A Mission (YWAM) campus in Tyler—and was going through their Discipleship Training School. Later she took a mission trip to New Orleans during Mardi Gras.

Near the end of our conversation that night, I asked her if I could see her sometime out at the ranch.

"Sure. I'll buy you an ice cream when you come by," she said.

Second Chapter got real busy after that night and went on the road for some time. When I got around to looking Deanne up, I found out that she had finished her schooling and gone back to Rockford. I wondered if I would ever see her again.

Twin Oaks Ranch had a gymnasium in which they held Sunday morning services. I began attending church there regularly, and about a year after I had met Deanne, guess who showed up one Sunday morning? After the service was over, I walked up to her and said, "You owe me an ice cream."

She looked at me in surprise and said, "Very good memory."

I mustered up my courage and said, "Would you like to go out with me sometime?"

"Well, there's this new movie I'd like to see, but I'm afraid to ask anyone at the base to go because of the rating."

"What's the movie?"

"An Officer and a Gentleman."

I thought it sounded like a chick flick, but I was looking for any excuse to see her, so I said, "Sure."

After our first date, I knew Deanne was someone I could talk to for hours on end. We began to see each other often. My brother Jack and I had an apartment together in the metal Second Chapter building my family had built to house our ministry. This apartment soon became one of Deanne's and my favorite hangouts. Some nights we'd stay up late talking and really getting to know each other. One day as Second Chapter was getting ready to leave on tour, I asked her if there was any possibility our relationship would go any deeper than just friends.

"Absolutely not," she said.

That came as a surprise to me because I thought we'd been developing feelings for each other. *Oh well.*

The tour was much like many others, except that on this one I met a girl I thought might be the one for me. The tour ended, and when I saw Deanne again, I told her that I had something I needed to say to her. She said she had something to tell me as well, but she asked me to go first. After I finished telling her about this girl I had met, she said, "Well, I've changed my mind about my feelings for you. I think I care for you more than I thought."

Now I had no idea what I was supposed to do.

Deanne said to me, "I think you need to figure out if these feelings you have for this other girl are worth pursuing. I want you to make the right choice."

So I made arrangements to see the other girl in Arizona.

I stayed with her and her family for a few days. I was having some serious doubts about the whole thing when out of the blue the phone rang and it was Deanne looking for me. You couldn't have imagined the shock I felt when I went to the phone and heard her voice on the other end. I had not given Deanne this girl's phone number, and I was stumped as to how she had tracked me down. (She told me later that she had found my phone bill and looked up the area code, and she was off to the races.) We spoke for a few minutes, and during the course of our conversation, I became more and more aware that I was in the wrong place and needed to return home.

When I got off the phone, I had to tell this girl in Arizona how I felt. It was an incredibly awkward and uncomfortable conversation, but when I was done explaining what had happened, she was very understanding (thank God).

After I arrived back home, Deanne and I saw each other a lot. My feelings for her grew more romantic, and I found myself looking forward more eagerly to our times together. It wasn't long before I knew I had it bad.

At the time, Deanne had a job at a day-care center run by YWAM. Many times I would visit her at work, since I wasn't happy with the thought of seeing her only at night. One day, while I was spending time with her at the day care, I had an overwhelming desire to ask her to marry me. It wasn't something I had been thinking about; it just sort of popped out. Not only did the words surprise *me,* but Deanne never saw it coming either. At first she asked if I was serious, then after a few moments, she looked up at me and said yes.

Since I Found You

My family no doubt had an inkling that I was seeing someone, but they had no idea it was serious. I had kept the details about Deanne and me to myself. In fact, when I told Annie and Buck that I was engaged, they said, "To whom?" I think they were so used to being included in everything I did that they couldn't believe I had left them out of such an important decision. My thinking at the time was that I wanted to fall in love and make my romantic choice outside the family dynamic. I wanted Deanne to marry *me,* not my family.

Looking back, I realize I could have saved Deanne and me some grief if I had handled the situation differently. It wasn't fair to Deanne the way I threw her into my family like I did. Buck and Annie checked her out big time. I understood where they were coming from, considering that they were my second mom and dad. They were looking out for my best interests. But it was still uncomfortable.

Some family members (who will remain nameless) tried to discourage Deanne and me from getting married, hurting us badly in the process. I'm sure they were doing what they felt was right, but they hadn't had a chance to know this woman I had fallen in love with. I'm grateful that my family finally recognized Deanne for who she was and came to understand and appreciate my love for her. Today my family thinks the world of her.

Deanne and I were engaged for six months. We went through all the typical feelings during those months. Because of the way some of my family members had reacted to news of our engagement, Deanne had some serious doubts about our future together. She actually called off our marriage twice during that time. Each time, I talked her back into marrying me (I wasn't about to lose the best thing that had ever happened to me), though it took a little more convincing each time.

The wedding day finally came: September 3, 1983. Bridesmaids and groomsmen flew in from all over, along with friends Deanne or I had grown up with. My best man was my brother Jack. We didn't have a huge wedding—just two hundred of our close friends.

The wedding was held outside, in a field belonging to yet another of the Christian ministries in the area—Agape Force. We chose it because it was a beautiful place and had facilities for our reception. The ceremony began at ten in the morning, but it was already hot. East Texas weather is still brutal that time of year, especially when you're wearing a tux.

As the ceremony got under way, my brother Frank and my sister Nellie (who had gotten married herself a few years earlier) were sitting next to each other, crying their eyes out. For some reason, I found that comical. You would have thought, by watching them, that there had been a death in the family. However, I wasn't much better, as I was crying too.

Prior to the big event, Annie and I had written a beautiful wedding song. (I wish we had recorded it, because now it's gone forever.) The plan was for me to sing the song during the ceremony, but I was too emotional to do it. Deanne was disappointed, but I made up for it by singing the song during the reception.

After the wedding, Deanne and I left late in the day for Houston. We spent our first night together there before heading out the next morning for our honeymoon in the Bahamas.

Tornado Alley

Back home in Texas, Deanne and I started setting up house. Before our honeymoon, we had purchased a single-wide trailer that we situated on a portion of Second Chapter's hundred acres of land. We believed we were being prudent with our finances, but as it turned out, that was not true.

First, we needed a well to supply the trailer with water. (We didn't get city water to that spot for a couple of years.) By the time we dug deep enough to find water, coupled with having to build a shed for the tanks and pumps and so on, we were out more than seven thousand dollars. Not to mention the costs for running electrical lines.

Now, picture this. Once we got all the necessary things in place, we moved in, only to find that our new well was pumping out the most disgusting-tasting water imaginable. At this point we spent another ton of money for a filter that was supposed to get rid of all impurities. The iron levels in the water were so high, though, that the filter worked for only a brief time before it clogged. After going round and round with the filter company, we ended up bypassing the filter and using the water only for bathing. We had to haul our drinking water from a different source. It grew almost comical after a while as our toenails and hair started taking on an orange hue because of the iron.

Buying that trailer was the worst financial decision I've ever made. I used to say that God must hate mobile homes. It seemed that every time I'd watch the news during tornado season, I would see images of a trailer park reduced to a pile of sticks. Living where we did in East Texas, in an area commonly referred to as Tornado Alley, I was always mindful of the weather.

During the middle of one tornado season, Deanne decided to take our firstborn, Megin, and visit her grandparents in Florida. One evening while she was gone, a terrific storm came through our neck of the woods. As I sat alone in the trailer, I heard the wind picking up outside and felt the trailer rocking. I was watching an old black-and-white movie when all of a sudden the power went out.

Our mobile home had a metal roof that amplified the sound of the rainfall. Normally I rather enjoyed this drumming effect, especially late at night when I was going to sleep. But this night it served more as an early warning system. As I went to retrieve a flashlight, I noticed a sudden eerie hush that was quickly followed by a loud noise I've heard described by countless victims of tornadoes: the roar of an oncoming train.

With flashlight in hand, I headed for the door. The difference in air pressure between the inside of the trailer and outside was so great that as soon as I opened the door my ears popped and the door was ripped from my grasp. (Later I realized the door opened with such force that it shattered against the outside wall.) I'd seen enough footage of destroyed mobile homes to know that I didn't want to stay inside.

As the sound of the "train" grew louder, I stood on my deck, momentarily stunned, not sure what my next move should be. (I thought of jumping over the rail of my deck, to seek out a low spot. I'm glad I didn't, because by daybreak I saw that a large tree had been knocked down right where I would have landed.) Instead of jumping into darkness, I quickly worked my way across the deck and down the stairs. As soon as I reached the bottom, the winds' fury rapidly subsided, so I went to check on some friends, Chris and Judy Snell, who had a trailer near ours. With the morning light, Chris and I drove around to check out the surrounding area.

The winds had hit the Last Days property the hardest. The tornado had ripped off part of the corrugated metal roof on the house belonging to Melody Green (Keith's widow), and as the metal flew, it had cut through the power lines serving much of the area, including our mobile home. In the yard of a dentist who lived across the street from Melody, the winds had uprooted an old oak tree, flipped it over, and shoved it back down in the hole it had come from, with the root system sticking straight up in the air. A car at Last Days had been lifted over a wooden fence and then set back down in a field right side up and without a scratch on it—there were no tire tracks and no opening in the fence large enough for the car to have been driven through.

I started thinking about how close the main destructive force of that tornado had come to my mobile home. After doing some line-of-sight calculations, a chill ran through me as I realized that the funnel cloud had passed within two hundred yards of my trailer while I was inside it.

Moving to Town

Though I liked living on the Second Chapter property, after the experience with the tornado, I had a desire to get my family out of the trailer and into something more substantial. Not only was the trailer a box of sticks waiting to crumble, but it was also just too small for me. I'd get out of the shower with my orange toenails and try to brush what little hair I had left, only to smack my hand on the light fixture over my head. I'd walk down the narrow hallway, and my foot would bash into the trim work, which sent wood pieces flying all over the house.

One day, while walking in our woods, I began praying about moving into a home somewhere in the area. I felt the Lord telling me that He would make a way for us to move out only when we found out we were pregnant with our second child. But I didn't tell Deanne this right away because I didn't think she would be thrilled with the idea of being pregnant right then.

Some months had passed since my earnest prayer to move. One day our bank president called us with some information about a house under foreclosure. (I had asked him to keep an eye open for any good deals on a house.) He knew what the house should go for and extended a line of credit to us that, depending on how high the bids got, should cover it.

I was excited about the prospects of getting into a home, but I was faced with a dilemma. I remembered what I felt the Lord had said about the conditions of our move. The morning came for us to go down to the courthouse and begin the bidding procedures. Just before we were ready to leave, Deanne walked up to me and said, "Guess what."

I bit. "What?"

"We're pregnant."

My jaw just about hit the floor. I told her what the Lord had spoken to me about our moving, and we both got goose bumps. With a spring in our step, we went down to the courthouse, and to our surprise, we were the only ones who showed up for the bidding. Our bank president said how much he'd like to get for the house; I offered a dollar over that amount, and the house was ours.

Family Man

We lived in Hide-A-Way Lake, Texas, partway between Lindale and the Second Chapter property, for more than ten years. While in that house, we

Fish in a Basket

One time when my daughter Mattie was very young, she came up to the deck in front of our house where I was cleaning some fish and asked if she could have one to stick in her bicycle basket. She wanted to give a fish a ride around the community.

You should have seen what that looked like. The fish was way too big for her basket—it hung out both sides and flopped around as she pedaled. The looks on the neighbors' faces were priceless as she wheeled her fish by their yards.

had two more children. I wrote a lot of songs there, perfected the art of fishing for bass, changed a lot of diapers, went through struggles with cancer and depression, and was assistant coach for Megin's baseball team.

While there are probably many things in life one can never be fully ready for, two that stand out to me are marriage and child rearing. I've heard marriage described as a collision of two histories, and I suppose that's true enough. But for me, being a father has hands-down been the most difficult task I've ever undertaken.

When I think back on my childhood, having been the youngest of nine siblings, I give my mom and dad a lot of grace. My circumstances were unusual because of my mom's illness, but in spite of her never being 100 percent physically during my childhood, she did quite a job of giving what she had.

I have relied on the power of prayer to get me through many parenting situations. My prayers, primarily, have been that the Lord would give me wisdom, discernment, revelation, and the ability to listen to my children. I learn more and more every day about what it means to truly listen to and understand where my children are coming from and (I hope) to give them wise counsel.

Our daughter Megin was born in 1985, Morgan in 1988, and Mattie in 1989. I can vividly remember them as toddlers and as very young kids doing and saying all the normal things. Like most parents, I thought that what my children did at any stage in their development was just amazing and that other children never did those things any better or any cuter. The funny thing is, even though that may not be true, I still *believe* it is.

I see my children through my father filter—and always will.

_12_

Second Chapter: Final Act

On August 12, 1988, I arrived at Sam Houston Coliseum in Houston, Texas, and as the equipment truck was unloaded, I started doing what I usually did before a Second Chapter of Acts concert—walked around the auditorium and prayed over the seats in expectation of what the Lord would do that night.

However, I knew the evening's concert would be unlike any other we had ever done: it would be our last.

I quickly found that it was impossible for me to go about my preparations with a business-as-usual attitude. My mind was pondering the fact that, after spending so many years on the road with my family, the ride was about to end. It was really all over.

The Edge of an End

Second Chapter had been touring in the United States and abroad for seventeen years. We were still as much in demand for concerts, if not more so. In fact, we had recently released our best-selling CDs ever, our collections of hymns. But we all agreed that it was time to quit. In part, this was because of the next generation of children coming up.

Nellie had married Steve Greisen in 1978, and now they were traveling with their two sons, Andrew and Jesse. The boys were getting older, and the thought of taking school-age children on the road didn't appeal to either Steve or Nellie. Meanwhile, Deanne and I had recently had our second daughter, Morgan. Our first daughter, Megin, was three. We were facing the same kinds of challenges in raising children on the road as Nellie and Steve.

But while our children's getting older was one of the factors in deciding to stop touring, it wasn't the most important one: we all felt that the Lord was calling us to quit. Years earlier, much to our surprise, He had put us together as a singing group. And now He was just as much in control in telling us that this season was over—Second Chapter had done what it was supposed to do.

So as 1988 approached, we knew this would be our last year.

We didn't go the route so many other groups had taken, making hoopla out of impending retirement. As a matter of fact, some of our loyal fans were upset with us when they found out we wouldn't be coming through their towns anymore: "If we had known you were quitting, we would have come to see you," some of them said. Over the years, we had been non-self-promoting, perhaps to a fault, and that continued right to the end.

As the date for the last official concert approached, it became obvious that it would be an emotional event. Houston, over the years, had proved to be one of our better-attended concerts; the night of August 12, 1988, was no exception. Seventy-five hundred people packed Sam Houston Coliseum. We did our concert just like always, but we could feel something different in the air.

As we sang, I began to see in my mind's eye vignettes of past concerts and experiences we'd had together. I began recalling other Christian artists we had performed with over the years, groups and performers such as Love Song, J. C. Power Outlet, Children of the Light, Randy Stonehill, Andraé Crouch, and Phil Keaggy. On and on it went.

Then, as the images continued, they morphed from the groups we had sung with to images of people the Lord had touched through all the concerts. I saw the faces of people who had been delivered from demonic oppression, people who had been healed from one kind of illness or another, many who had called upon the name of the Lord for freedom in different areas of life. It was almost more than I could bear. I realized that something far greater than the sum of our parts was coming to a close, something the Lord Himself had knit together for the glory of His name, something so wonderful that there will be no way of knowing just what God has done through us until we stand before Him in heaven.

After so many years together, seeing God move in such remarkable ways, it was almost impossible for me to come to grips with the finality of it all. As the last notes of the concert died away, Nellie looked over at me with a look in her eyes I wasn't used to seeing. It was as if with this one glance she said, "Wow! All those years, all those miles, all those miracles—we are standing on the edge of an end as well as a beginning."

A big Christian radio station in Houston, KSBJ, usually helped sponsor and promote our concerts when we came to town. When we finished singing, DJ Tom Dooley from the station asked us to stay onstage so he could present us with a plaque commemorating our many years together. As the plaque was given and Dooley explained its meaning, the crowd erupted in applause. Up to that point, I had honestly thought I'd be able to hold it together—and so far I had. But then I looked over at Annie and saw tears in her eyes. That did me in. Tears filled my eyes as well.

The Cruise from Hell

That concert in Houston was Second Chapter's last regular concert, but it wasn't absolutely our final performance as a group. There were two other times when we got together to sing for an audience. The first time came shortly after the Houston concert when we performed aboard a cruise ship.

If the Houston concert was a spiritual and emotional high point, the cruise was the pits.

We had recently finished a CD called *Far Away Places,* and our record label thought it would be cool to have a contest in which the winners got to go on a cruise with Second Chapter to faraway places (get it?). The cruise started in Tampa Bay, Florida, and traveled along Mexico's Yucatán peninsula, stopping at such spots as Cancún and Cozumel. It had a Christian theme, and Second Chapter was the big draw, at least for the Christians on board. Little did we know that among ourselves this trip would quickly earn the name "the cruise from hell."

When we showed up at the port in Florida and I got my first glimpse of the ship, I instantly had feelings of trepidation. I had never been on a cruise before, but even I could tell the ship had seen better days. It looked ancient, with scrapes and scratches and patches of rust. What were we getting ourselves in for?

The first glitch occurred when the ship's staff refused to allow our band to load instruments and other equipment onto the ship. It had something to do with weight restrictions or space aboard the ship, I believe. Buck argued the point, but to no avail. In the end, we decided that we would just make the best of it and do some sort of unplugged music sets.

As we pulled away from the dock and I made my way around the ship, I could tell something was up. I overheard people talking about one of the organizers of the cruise bailing off the ship because it had been overbooked.

Not long after that, the cruise line had to off-load some passengers and ferry them back to shore. I'm sure they were reimbursed, but what a drag it must have been to plan a vacation and go to the trouble and expense of getting to Tampa Bay, only to find out you weren't allowed to go.

As the cruise got under way, we all settled into our cabins (and I use the term "cabins" loosely). The space Deanne and I were assigned was so incredibly tiny that we could hardly find a spot for our luggage. Our shower was so small that I had to hang parts of my anatomy outside as I bathed others.

A collapsible wall was the only thing separating our cabin from Buck

Little Darling

Our daughter Megin, born in 1985, spent her infant and toddler years on the road. Some of Megin's first words were "auditorium" and "hotel." She pronounced auditorium as "awdeetoeweeum." She always put the second word in the form of a question: "Hotel we are?"

Megin was a terribly cute kid, with blond ringlets flowing down each side of her face. One time my sister Annie took Megin to the back of the bus for a while, and when they came out, we saw that Annie had dressed her in a big hat and scarf, complete with high heels and way too much makeup. She had also given her a candy cigarette (thanks so much, Annie) and had her walk the aisle of the bus like an old movie actress—one hand on her hip, the other holding the cigarette, waving the candy cigarette about while saying in an exaggerated voice, "Dahling."

and Annie's. Talk about lack of privacy. Buck would wake up a lot earlier than Deanne or I, and we could plainly hear him making his coffee. The only plus about that in the morning was that Buck made enough coffee for everyone—and he always made the best coffee.

From the time we came on board the ship until we got off, Deanne was seasick. She tried to make the best of it but was miserable the whole time.

And that was not all Deanne had to put up with. Every time she would walk by herself somewhere on the ship, she would be approached by male employees of the cruise line who had other things on their minds besides work. I soon decided to accompany her wherever she went.

When it came time for Second Chapter to sing, I was reminded of our early performances together, thanks to the bad lighting, poor sound system, and funky stage. We had been reduced to a few microphones and a lame excuse for a keyboard. Still, we made the best of a bad situation, and I think the audience appreciated that in spite of being severely limited, we gave it our all.

Mercifully, we got through our musical obligation, and we tried our best to enjoy what the ship had to offer.

One evening I was watching a movie in the lower part of the ship and felt a wave of nausea sweep over me. I made a mad dash to get topside, because I thought for sure I was going to blow, but as soon as I saw the horizon and took a few deep breaths of fresh air, the feeling of nausea disappeared. I've been on a few ships since then, but that was the closest I have ever come to being seasick.

On another night we were at dinner—it was one of the nights when we were supposed to dress up—and everything was going along fine when all of a sudden we heard an argument break out in the kitchen between one of the waiters and a chef. After a few moments, the argument escalated into quite a fight. We could hear the two of them yelling at the top of their lungs in what sounded like Spanish and the sound of dishes being thrown around and smashing. Nearing the apex of the fight, one of the pair brandished a knife and went after the other. It concluded with the attacker being tossed in the brig until we reached the next port of call, where he was arrested and taken ashore.

I vowed never to go on another cruise as long as I lived. I thought that if all cruises were this weird, I'd just as soon take a pass. (I held to my commitment for many years, though eventually I took my oldest daughter, Megin, on a cruise to Alaska, which we both enjoyed immensely.)

Diving the Plane

Not all the memories I have about the cruise are bad ones. Several of my brothers and their wives came along, as did many of our friends, making the experience much more tolerable. Among our friends were Chris and Judy Snell. Chris had not only helped build our ministry headquarters, but he had also become one of our equipment managers (a fancy way of saying "roadie"). He had traveled with us for years and become one of my best friends.

I had heard that Cozumel had some of the best snorkeling in the world, so when we arrived at the island, I got Chris and my brothers Tony and Jack to join me in that venture. It took us no time at all to find a place that rented snorkeling gear.

Before donning my face mask and fins, I covered every exposed part of my body with waterproof sunblock. I had learned over the years, through some painful experiences in Florida and Hawaii, that it paid for me to put on large quantities of sunblock before spending time in the water. It wasn't hard to convince my brothers to join me in lathering up, but Chris said something to the effect that he didn't burn easily. I tried to tell him that the sun there was more brutal than what we were used to, but he shrugged off the warning.

Once we got in the water and our face masks went below the surface, we instantly saw color, most of which had gills and fins attached. Other than when snorkeling in Hawaii, I had never seen so many beautiful fish. We swam close to shore for some time, enjoying the underwater scene. Then the four of us made our way to a sunken plane that the man who rented us the snorkeling gear had told us about. Apparently the plane had been dropped into the ocean for no other reason than to give scuba divers something to explore. And sure enough, as we watched from above, a number of scuba divers were going into, around, and through the plane.

We pulled the snorkels out of our mouths and sized up the situation. We all agreed that the plane was a good forty or more feet below the surface. But for as long as I could remember, my brother Tony had always been the first to try something if he thought he had even a small chance of success, and now I could see the wheels spinning in his head. Oh no, I could tell he was seriously considering making a free dive to the plane.

My mental wheels were spinning as well. Ever since the days of hanging out at the American River in California with my brothers, I had loved swimming. At our home in Texas, we had an Olympic-sized swimming pool where I was able to swim underwater for a lap and a half. I had also done a lot more free diving in the ocean than any of the others and had some idea of what it would take to make it down to the plane with nothing more than the air I carried in my lungs. So as they were discussing the dive, I had already started to hyperventilate in anticipation of the dive— for once in my life I wasn't going to let Tony beat me to the punch. As they talked it over, I said something like, "See ya," then took one last breath and began the descent.

As I swam downward, the pressure built up in my ears. I knew enough to pinch my nose and blow to equalize the pressure. Getting nearer the plane, I began to wonder whether I was going to have enough air to make it back up. But I finally touched the wing of the plane—my goal—and headed back to the surface as quickly as possible.

I could tell that the others were more than a little surprised that I had taken the first plunge. But once they saw that it was doable, they each took off for the plane. When some scuba divers showed up to check out the plane, I could tell they were annoyed that we were making the dive without the expense and trouble of all the scuba gear. We also had the distinct impression that we were somehow invading their space.

Overall, the time we spent snorkeling was a blast. We did, however, run into a couple of problems. On one of the last dives, my brother Tony (who knew better) allowed his face mask to create an unusual amount of suction to his face. I guess he didn't equalize the pressure soon enough. When he surfaced, we noticed that he had broken capillaries around his eyes. By the time we made it back to the ship, we could see the extent of the damage—his eyes looked like something from a sci-fi movie. It took a week or two for his eyes to heal.

The other problem stemmed from Chris's opting not to wear sunblock. Naturally, when you snorkel, you spend the majority of your time with your back toward the sun as you swim facedown. Chris was wearing a T-shirt, and because he had worked in construction most of his life, his arms and neck were okay. However, he was wearing shorts, which left the backs of his legs completely exposed. He normally wore long pants when he worked, and so the skin on his legs had not seen that much sun. I have never seen a worse sunburn in my life. The backs of Chris's legs ended up looking like a cross between beef jerky and leather that had been tanned too long. His skin got so tight that it was all he could do just to get around.

Tom Jones's Brother

The cruise included an interesting mix of people. Though there were many Christians on board, it was far from being a Christians-only cruise. And that meant it was an odd environment, as you could be praying with some-one one second, then take a few steps and come across a couple making out like dogs in heat, then take a few more steps and see a table full of people drinking themselves into oblivion. It's not that I'm a prude; I've been around weird stuff all my life. It was just strange to see so plainly the line between darkness and light.

We were not the only entertainers on board either. One guy, a regular performer aboard the ship, claimed to be the brother of the Welsh crooner Tom Jones. I had no reason to doubt him, as he looked and sounded like the brother he laid claim to. But I was never quite certain.

One night, while Tom's sibling was performing onstage, I sat in the back of the room and listened as he sang his rendition of "What's New, Pussycat?" (whoa, whoa). I watched as half the room ignored him, carry-ing on their conversations as if he weren't even there, and the other half of the room drank themselves silly, more than likely with a buzz inside their heads louder than brother-of-Tom's song.

As the crooner was finishing his set, I realized how blessed I'd been over the years. It was a humbling moment to understand how the Lord had seen fit to raise up three self-conscious, insecure, and scared people to reach so many others with His life, hope, and love. We had been blessed as a group to have crowds of people not only who wanted to hear us but also who were, for the most part, willing to allow the Lord to minister to them through what He had given us. I saw clearly a picture of our small beginnings, how the Lord used our own brokenness to create vessels willing to be used in pouring out His oil.

Supposedly, some years after our hellish cruise, the ship we sailed on caught fire and sank. I don't know whether that's true or not, but I sure can believe it. As long as no one got hurt, that was a fitting end to that dilapidated old bucket of rust.

The Roar of Love

The only other thing Second Chapter did together after the cruise was a brief series of performances in December 1993. Eastside Foursquare Church, in Bothell, Washington, was putting on a live production based on C. S. Lewis's popular fantasy novel *The Lion, the Witch and the Wardrobe*. Because years before we'd recorded *The Roar of Love,* an album based on that book, the church thought it would be great to have us come out onstage from time to time and sing songs that fit the different scenes throughout the play. We had never sung most of the *Roar of Love* songs live, so it was fun to see how the music enhanced the story.

After so many years of our not singing together, it amazed me how quickly we found our musical center and made the songs sound like we had done them a hundred times before. We ended up doing nine shows, with the stipulation that the church couldn't advertise the fact that Second Chapter was involved. After all, we were singing as a favor to the church, not because the group was really back together again. But it didn't take long for word to leak out, and even though the church stayed true to its commitment not to mention us in their promotion, all nine events sold out.

I felt good about that being the last time we sang together, because the event was so well accepted and about twenty thousand people got to hear it. I had always believed that *The Roar of Love* was one of our best efforts. It was ahead of its time. Unfortunately, it also proved, from a sales standpoint, to be one of our best-kept secrets. I'm pleased to say that a spillover effect from Walt Disney Pictures' 2005 movie based on Lewis's book has been that our collection *The Roar of Love* has found new listeners.

As a matter of fact, all our CDs are still being purchased and listened to, touching people's hearts, even though Second Chapter has not sung together in public for more than a decade.

I still get a kick out of hearing from people who have been impacted by our music over the years. Some of the stories are amazing. Like the old woman who was in a coma and dying when her daughter put headphones on her ears and played "Holy, Holy, Holy" (from our hymns collection) for her. Though the old woman had been unconscious for some time, at the end of the song she opened her eyes and whispered, "That was beautiful!" and then died peacefully.

Thank You, God, for creating and sustaining Second Chapter of Acts.

13

Going Solo

On that night of the last performance at Sam Houston Coliseum, I had no idea what was around the corner for me. And that was difficult to deal with, since so much of my life to that point had been plainly laid out.

I soon discovered that God had much more in mind. After years of being the "little brother," I was about to see how God would use me in a solo career.

Long before Second Chapter concluded, I started doing solo albums. Though I loved Annie's writing, I felt that a different expression of music needed to surface through my own creative endeavors. My style had a harder edge than most of the material Annie wrote.

While still touring with Second Chapter, I recorded three solo records. I would open the second half of our concerts with a short set of songs from my newest release. This arrangement worked well for me, because I really didn't want to add more touring, and I could use our existing band, sound system, and lights. It was nice to have a large audience to hear a sampling of my latest stuff too.

All this laid a solid groundwork for the solo career I have had since Second Chapter ended. As of the time this book went to press, I had recorded eight solo records, with plans to do more. And while I've not done extensive touring like Second Chapter did, I have made many shorter trips to sing as a solo act.

It all started back nearly at the beginning of my professional music career.

Toward Eternity

I began work in 1976 on my first solo album, which ended up being called *Toward Eternity.* That recording originally was called *Matthew 18,* a take-off on "Second Chapter of Acts," as well as an attempt at humor because that was my name and age. The problem was I didn't finish the album until I was twenty-one.

Toward Eternity was amazing to me, not just because it was my first record, but because of all the twists and turns it took before we finished.

Michael Omartian was slated to produce the album. We'd known Michael for years, and he had worked in some capacity on most of Second Chapter's early recordings. Michael's a musical genius, and I was honored to work with him.

As I mentioned before, I've always loved laying down tracks in the studio. This recording was no exception. At the time I was a real Stevie Wonder fan, so I was pumped to find out that my session's bass player was Scotty Edwards who had played on several of Stevie's early hits. Equally impressive to me were some of the other players—on guitar Ray Parker Jr. (who I loved), Phil Keaggy (what a monster), and Jay Graydon (who later turned into quite a producer himself).

After my first tracking date, though, Michael approached Buck and me and said, "I don't think Matt's ready to do a solo record."

That took me aback, so I asked him, "Why?"

"I just don't think you're mature enough," Michael said.

At the time I was put out by his comments and believed that his reasons were too vague. But in the end I decided that maybe it was for the best to wait a while. A couple of years went by, and I could see no reason to wait any longer. I pressed Michael to get started, but he always seemed to have an excuse for not proceeding with my solo project. I was young and not so patient. I may be wrong, but at the time I felt that I was getting the runaround. Michael was becoming a much-in-demand producer. Why should he produce the likes of me when he was producing artists like Jermaine Jackson? So Buck and I came to the conclusion that we shouldn't wait any longer. He would produce the album.

Buck and I had a great time doing *Toward Eternity.* We picked songs together and talked about direction. Two songs were by Keith Green—"Summer Snow" and "Gotta Do Better than This." Annie wrote several for the project, and Phil Keaggy contributed "Noah's Song."

When it came time to record Keith's songs, we asked him if he would play piano on the session. He agreed, and some years after Keith had died, I listened again to "Summer Snow" and recalled Keith in the studio, beating on the keys, rocking back and forth as he laid down his piano parts. It really made me miss him.

Phil Keaggy, who by then had become a good friend, ended up recording many of the electric and acoustic parts, as well as all the guitar solos. Very nice.

My first solo album was unique in that all production costs were covered before it even hit the stores. When Billy Ray knew I would do a record for him, he began to presell into stores. Because *Toward Eternity* took three years to finish, Billy had time to take preorders for a bunch of records. That's how we paid off the production costs before it was released in 1979.

And that first album kind of spoiled me too. I got paid royalties right away and didn't have to wait for the album to recoup production costs. The first royalty check came and had some nice numbers on it—even without the greatest math skills I could tell that. *Ah, so this is what I like about the recording business,* I thought.

Armed and Dangerous

I wasn't exactly in a hurry to advance my solo career: Another seven years passed before my second album, *Armed and Dangerous,* was ready. All the songs on it were written by the Second Chapter keyboard player, Jim Tenneboe, or me. This project was different in several ways from my first album. We incorporated much of the new technology that was available at the time, such as digital sampling and keyboard sequencing.

I thought long and hard about who I wanted to play on the record and came up with a list of players who blew me away. After the first tracking date, I knew I was onto something special.

The drummer was a guy I'd listened to for years—Mike Beard. I loved his hard-hitting, meat-and-potatoes style of playing. But he wasn't a Christian, and I knew that might affect the dynamic of the recording.

When it came time to record Mike's tracks, I picked him up in Dallas, and on the ride back to the studio he asked me if the project was Christian. I told him yes. He didn't say anything more about it at the time, but he explained to me later that he was envisioning hokey music and was thinking, *What have I gotten myself into?* He ended up being pleasantly surprised by the quality of stuff we did.

Even though Mike was more than a little rough around the edges, my philosophy was different from most other Christian artists at the time. I figured, what could it hurt to have this guy play on something that might speak to his life? Also, I simply wanted the best, and I didn't know of any Christian drummers at the time who could pull off what I wanted.

I told Mike that I loved what he'd done for all the Mike Post television themes, as well as all the Rick Springfield stuff he'd done. I think I surprised Mike with my knowledge of his recording career, and that may have caused him to see me in a different light. Maybe I wasn't as big a dork as he had at first believed.

I recorded that album quite differently from anything else I'd done to that point. Instead of having all the players record their parts at once and fix little problems afterward, I took a more microscopic approach and recorded musicians separately. The first thing we laid down were sequenced keyboards (synthesizers that had their parts played perfectly by computer) and a sampled bass part that the drummer would play to later. Once we had the keys, bass, and drums recorded, I brought in guitar and other instruments as needed. As was normally the case, we would record the lead vocals, background vocals, and any other additional parts, such as guitar overdubs or strings, last.

As we readied ourselves to record the drums, Mike asked Greg Hunt (the engineer) and me if we wanted him to play with the bass, or should he lock in with the click (the metronome that was keeping time for us)? This comment caught me off guard, because I didn't realize there was any difference between the two. Mike went on to explain some technical stuff about MIDI delay and said that there were a few milliseconds separating bass from click. I told Mike to play with the bass.

When Mike started recording, I'd never heard a drummer play so hard. I went into the studio to listen—big mistake. It was so loud my ears hurt. I had to leave the room.

A few days after we recorded the drums, I flew the guitar player in to record his parts. Dan Huff had been recommended by a friend of mine, and he ended up being one amazing guitar player. Normally, guitar players seem to do best with very specific instructions on their parts, but Dan often would look at me and say, "Nice part. How about if I incorporate your idea with this?" Then he would start playing a part that had some of the elements I'd asked for but was usually far superior. Dan had a wonderful ability to microproduce himself. He and Phil Keaggy are the most musically intuitive guitar players I've worked with.

Armed and Dangerous was my first attempt at producing, and I enjoyed it immensely.

Greg

I mentioned that the recording engineer on *Armed and Dangerous* was Greg Hunt, owner of Rosewood Studios, located in Tyler, Texas. Through the years, Greg engineered all but one of my solo records. To say that he and I became good friends would be a complete understatement. We've spent thousands of hours together in that studio, not counting all the time on fishing trips and so on.

When I first met Greg, I was new to the South and not used to hanging out with people who spoke with a Southern accent. Greg's drawl made me think he was a country bumpkin, but it didn't take long for me to change my opinion of him. I learned he had designed and built the whole studio structure, and I was impressed as he unfolded his knowledge of acoustic engineering.

Greg was a master at recording acoustic instruments. You could hear his years of experience shine through when he recorded acoustic guitar, mandolin, banjo—any instrument with strings attached to it.

Another of his fortes was capturing drum sounds. He really knew his room and the best places to set up drum kits. I would sit behind the sound board while he went into the studio. The drummer would play as Greg made small adjustments in microphone placement. He would then look at me through the soundproof glass and wait until I gave him the thumbs-up. Next, he'd come in and listen a moment while the drummer continued playing. After that, Greg and I would switch places: I'd go into the room and make slight adjustments until we agreed that we had found the best hot spots.

To me, Greg is a scientist of sound. When I first told Greg he was my favorite engineer, he gave me a disbelieving look. He knew I'd worked with some of the big names in LA and Nashville, so I'm sure he thought I was flattering him. A few years later, though, he was voted one of the top five

Superman

As part of my contract with Sparrow to record my first album, *Toward Eternity,* I wrote in that upon signing I would receive a full-size pinball machine of my choice (within reason, of course). That's the kind of thing an eighteen-year-old does, right?

The Superman movie was slated for the near future, and a pinball-machine manufacturer had decided to cash in on the Superman theme.

When I went shopping for my machine, I saw the Superman one and knew I had to have it. Billy Ray Hearn, the president of Sparrow, hemmed and hawed for a while, since the machine cost close to three thousand dollars. In the end, though, Billy Ray bought it for me.

I still have that pinball machine, but the long storage in Texas corroded the parts, and I doubt that the flippers would flip. But maybe one of these days, when I have some spare time...

recording engineers in the United States by *Mix* magazine. I wasn't the only one who thought Greg had special talent.

Home-Based Musician

After Second Chapter stopped touring in 1988, Nellie pretty much got out of music altogether. Annie, on the other hand, never slowed down. She just kept right on touring with her husband, Buck.

I wasn't at all sure what my next step should be. Everything I'd known, regarding work, had come to an end. Our second child, Morgan, was still a baby. Deanne and I had bought a house, and with all the new responsibility and no firm direction, I entered a bad bout with depression that lasted for several months. I guess you could say I had a nervous breakdown.

I found myself praying things like, *God, I need to hear from You in a fresh way*, and *Lord, I don't want to just continue in music because it's the easiest path—I want to know it's what You want from me.*

Slowly, I came out of my funk and began to do a few concerts here and there with other artists. Also, during this time, I started doing more producing. Greg Hunt, Gary Leach, and I produced eight or nine albums for different artists in those years.

Following the birth of my third daughter, Mattie, in 1989, I decided to try and stay home even more and help raise the kids.

Besides producing, I got heavily into jingle work—recording music for commercials. I'd never have considered doing commercial work in earlier years, but now I found that the work came easily to me, the people I worked with were fun, and the money was decent. Most important, jingle work meant I didn't have to travel so much.

With my decision to stay home more, I thought it would be a great opportunity for me to get into shape physically. I had done a lot of running some years earlier (something Phil Keaggy had gotten me into), but it had been a while since I ran and played racquetball and other sports. I had no real desire to pick up running again, so I decided to try cycling. Riding bikes was something I had always enjoyed, so I went to the local bike shop and picked out a mountain bike. I also still had my old Schwinn touring bike, which I got out of storage, tuned up, and started riding.

Even though I wasn't doing concerts during this time, I still recorded solo albums. As my girls grew older during the early 1990s, I decided it was time to pursue live concerts. But just as I was getting back into the swing of performing again, the bottom fell out of my life.

And I never saw it coming.

14

Uninvited Guest

In October of 1993 I knew something had gone haywire with my body.

I didn't think too much about it at first, because I'd experienced some similar problems before, and in time they always seemed to correct themselves. This time, however, the ailment didn't go away and grew worse.

When I concluded in the first week of December that I had to see a doctor, I was with Annie in Seattle, where we were doing some performances together. I told her something weird was up with me.

When I got back home from Seattle, I made an appointment in Tyler to see a urologist by the name of Dr. Roberts. The soonest he could see me was January 5, so I waited for several weeks, though I already knew in my gut that an operation would be inevitable. Before examining me, Dr. Roberts asked me several questions and finally said that more than likely he would find something simple like a cyst and that I shouldn't be worried. But when I told him that for a month and a half my breasts had been enlarged and tender, his expression instantly changed.

He checked me out and said, "This is not what I thought it was. You need to have this removed right away. What you have just described makes me believe it's hormonal, which may suggest that it could be testicular cancer." The doctor then told me there was no way he could tell exactly whether the growth was cancerous or benign, but he said it didn't look like it was going to get better on its own. He then asked me how I felt about undergoing surgery the next day.

"Let's go for it," I said,

Dr. Roberts called East Texas Medical Center in Tyler and set up a surgery slot.

This information sent me into a tailspin. I had never undergone surgery before, unless extraction of wisdom teeth counts. I suddenly had a bunch of phone calls to make to family and friends so they could be informed— and so they could pray! Of course, the upside to next-day surgery is that you hardly have time to worry about it.

Deanne and I (Chris and Judy Snell came too, for support) went to East Texas Medical in the morning for admission. A little while later, Pastor Tracy Hanson from our church, Community Christian Fellowship, arrived, and we all talked before he offered a wonderful prayer for me, which I greatly appreciated. Then some other friends showed up to hang out and talk with me before surgery. A nurse slipped an IV needle in my arm, and then an orderly arrived with a wheelchair to take me away for surgery prep. Before he wheeled me off, my friends gathered around me for a quick prayer.

After some chest x-rays, I met with my anesthesiologist. My cardiologist had been in touch with him and had expressed some concerns as to what type of anesthetic would be used. After we decided on what type, my anesthesiologist asked if he could pray for me before he began. That really blew me away, because I had been hoping to get another guy—a believer whom a friend of mine had for his surgery. Now here I was with a doctor who said he always tries to pray with his patients before he begins. The Lord was really looking out for me!

The surgery went well, and when I was coherent, the nurse told me I could go home as soon as I could urinate. Well, I never liked hospitals—they were the places you went when you died—so I couldn't wait to get out. I called the nurse and informed her that I thought I might be able to go. As I got off the bed, it was all I could do to keep from passing out. But after taking a couple of deep breaths, I made my way across the room and into the bathroom. I stood there, with the nurse listening on the other side of the door, until I could muster enough water works to satisfy her.

I had Chris get the car so it would be out front when the nurse wheeled me down in a wheelchair. As I began to get into the car, I could tell I was going out for the count. I knew if I were to pass out, the nurse wouldn't let me leave, so I grabbed the recline lever on the car seat and got it as close to prone as I could. Barely conscious, I waved at the nurse as I told Chris to hit the gas and get me out of there. From the time surgery had started, I spent only four and a half hours at the medical center

The day after surgery, I wasn't in much shape to do anything. I just lay in bed and stared at the ceiling. The doctor had told me to stay in bed for a few days, and for the first day I was happy to comply. By the third or fourth day, though, I was going stir-crazy. So I drove myself down to the dock and went fishing. Over the next three days, I must have caught fifty bass.

That first day fishing, I felt the Lord talking to me, and I expressed some feelings to the Lord too. This started to free me from my fears and concerns. At this point I didn't know the results of the pathology on my tumor, but I knew I'd be doing things differently from then on anyway, because I had become aware of the "nowness" of life. I knew as well that I would no longer feel so afraid of things that had always scared me, such as performing live (even after so many years of experience).

About the fifth day after surgery I got the pathology results. The tumor was very rare. Not only was it malignant, but it had three different types of cancer cells in it. While I was at Dr. Roberts's office getting the report, he made an appointment for me to have a CAT scan. So for the next few days I wandered around with my mind full of thoughts, things like *Am I going to be okay, or will they find tumors someplace else in my body?* During times like these, you find out in a hurry on whom you can depend—you either trust God to know what's best, or you freak out.

Recently I ran across a journal I thought was lost from January 28, 1994, about three weeks after I was diagnosed. As I reread the entries, my early reaction to cancer came back in all its freshness:

It's been three weeks and one day since my operation. Deanne thought it best for me to journal this before too much time has transpired. In looking back over that three-week span, it's amazing to me to realize all the emotional changes one person can go through. I spoke to my friend Dallas Holm about a week ago. [His wife, Linda, had recently gone through a bout with cancer.] One thing he told me—and I've found it to be true—is that so much of your life is reduced to five-minute chunks of information. Information that can leave you feeling relieved, concerned, and/or confused.

I had the CAT scan on a Friday, and early Saturday morning I had a very interesting impression. I felt like the Lord woke me up and spoke to me (not in an audible voice, but it was real to me just the same). This impression was, "I've healed you. It's going to be okay." It was a comforting moment for me, one full of reassurance and peace.

A few days later, while I was working in the studio, doing a soundtrack for a new Mercy Ships video, Ken Kummerfield (my cardiologist) called Deanne and told her that he had just run into my oncologist, who had told Ken that the CAT scans looked good, with no obvious signs of cancer spreading anywhere.

I finally met with my oncologist, Dr. Hyman, who at the end of my first appointment told me that though he could treat me, he felt I would get more up-to-date treatment if I went to M. D. Anderson Cancer Center in Houston. Dr. Hyman said, "They are doing stuff down there right now that I'll be reading about in medical journals seven months from now."

At M. D. Anderson, I met with Dr. Amatto. He looked at my case and thought it best for me to be placed in a program with about sixty other guys with the same type of cancer. After they ran more tests on me, Dr. Amatto told me I should consider chemotherapy, because he felt my blood work should have reflected a lower number of what they call tumor markers. That was a shocker to me, because I was expecting that they would just be monitoring me for some years, and that would be the end of it. I asked Dr. Amatto why I should do chemo, and he told me that according to the studies, guys who didn't do chemo had a 50 percent chance that the cancer would return. I said, "Okay, if I do the chemo, what is the rate of recurrence?"

He said, "It seems to drop to zero."

"Doc, if it were you, would you do the chemo?"

"Yes."

I was faced with an interesting decision. I'd always been a healthy guy, and now I was being asked to make myself intentionally sick. I wrestled with the decision for a few days, but in the end I decided to go for it.

Prep

For the next several weeks, I had blood drawn regularly in Tyler and shipped to Houston. On my next trip to Houston, a few days before they started chemo, the doctors did a procedure on me that I don't think they even perform anymore. They wanted to make sure that there wasn't anything going on in my body that the CAT scans might have missed. So I went through a procedure called a lymphangiogram, which allowed doctors to see on a more molecular level if I had cancer cells in my lymphatic system. This test was by far one of the most painful procedures I went through; the other painful procedure was when they put a "long line" in my arm for chemo. They had to inject my feet with blue dye, which they did by sticking a long needle between my toes. I asked why they had to do this, and the nurse said, "It's so there will be some contrast for us to find the clear vessel that leads to the rest of your lymphatic system."

Before the nurse began, she said something I've never heard a nurse say. She said, "Now, this is *really* going to hurt."

Man, she wasn't kidding. As she began, I broke out in a cold sweat. When she had finished with the first foot, she moved on to the second. She then went back to the first foot, injected some deadening agent in the top of one foot, then did the same to the other foot. After the tops of my feet were numb, she made a small incision in the top of each foot. Then she took a long metal instrument that had a small hook on one end and began rooting around, looking for the lymphatic vessel. Once she located it, she inserted a small needle into it and tied the needle to the vessel with a small piece of stitching. She repeated the procedure on the other foot. Then I had to lie there for an hour and a half while they slowly injected Iranian cottonseed oil into my lymphatic system.

I then needed to wait twenty-four hours for the cottonseed oil to penetrate my lymph glands. After I was scanned by a special machine, the tests came back negative.

Before they could start the chemo, they had to run some baseline tests on my lung capacity. One of the drugs they were going to give me was called Bleomyacin. This drug had a tendency to scar lung tissue. But doctors had learned that if they gave the drug in a twenty-four-hour infuser, that risk was greatly reduced. They normally wouldn't give the drug to older patients, because it had a tendency to kill them, so they wanted to make sure I was in good enough shape to handle it.

They took me into a room with machines to breathe into. One apparatus had a tube that was connected to a computer. They pinched off my nose with a clamp and asked me to take a deep breath and blow as hard as I could into the tube. I repeated the test three times so they could get an accurate reading. The averages for the three tests showed that for my age and weight, my lung capacity was 110 percent of normal.

One of the orderlies asked, "Why did you rate so high on that test?"

"Because I'm a distance cyclist and a singer."

"Oh," he said, "let me hear you sing something."

I thought it would be fun to sing "Amazing Grace," and because the guy was African American, I sang it as soulfully as I could. I closed my eyes and let it rip. The room I was in was small and had several doors that led to different rooms. When I finished singing, I opened my eyes to see that the room had filled with hospital workers who couldn't believe what they were hearing.

The orderly looked at me with his mouth hanging opened and said, "If I could sing like that, I'd never stop singing."

I got a big kick out of that.

What's really amazing about the whole thing is that I did that test on three different occasions—once before I started the chemo, again halfway through chemo, and finally when I'd finished chemo. With each test, my lung capacity grew: my second test went to 111 percent; the third, to 112 percent. The doctors had never seen that happen before. They informed me that in their previous experience lung capacity always diminished with that medication.

The next thing on the treatment prep list was to get my long line, which would allow the doctors to administer chemo without having to stick me every time. I went to another part of the hospital where the two women in charge asked me which arm I wanted the long line in.

I told them my right.

Then one of them asked, "Have you ever broken the collarbone on your right side."

I said, "No."

One of the nurses took some measurements of the distance between where the line was going in my arm to just before it reached my heart. At this point, one of them had me lie back and began to make a rather large incision (it seemed large to me) on the inside of my arm, just below where it bends at the elbow. Then she took a tube and began to insert it. As she snaked the tube into my arm, she kept telling me to relax, since she was having trouble getting it all the way in. I remember thinking, *Yeah, right. "Relax."* It hurt like the dickens.

After some effort, she finally got the line in place. Then I heard her say, "Oh no." In my experience, that phrase is not something you ever want to hear during a surgical procedure.

"What do you mean, 'Oh no'?" I asked her.

She said, "I can't get any blood flow from the tube." She then asked me if I'd ever suffered trauma to my right shoulder area.

"Yes."

Then she got kind of upset at me and said, "What kind of trauma?"

I told her that a few years earlier I'd had a bicycle accident, which resulted in my breaking my right scapula and separating my right shoulder.

"Why didn't you tell me that before I started?"

"Why on earth should I have told you about that?" I asked. "You asked me if I had ever broken my collarbone, and the answer was no."

She explained that the reason she couldn't get blood return from the line was because there must be some calcium deposits or scar tissue putting enough pressure on the line to restrict blood flow. So she took the line out and informed me without a hint of sympathy that she would have to do the whole painful procedure over again using the other arm.

To put it mildly, I was not a happy camper. But what choice did I have? After she began the process with my left arm, I realized that for some reason she was having an even harder time getting the tube through. Also, it was much more painful. Mercifully, once she finally got the tube in place for the second time, she got good blood return.

She then flushed the line out with saline, at which time I said, "Why did I hear that in my head?"

"You heard that in your head?" she asked.

"Yeah, when you flushed the line, I heard a noise in my head."

"Well, that's not a good sign."

She went on to explain that the tube might have taken the wrong turn. Instead of going into my chest, the goofy thing had gone up inside my neck. I'm lying there thinking, *Why can't things just go the way they're supposed to?* The only way to know where the tube was for sure was for me to go to another room, where they put me under a fluoroscope.

Even though what I'm about to describe was scary, I still found it quite fascinating. A doctor asked if I wanted to watch what he was about to do, and I said, "Yeah, I'd love to watch." He positioned a screen so I could see a type of x-ray that is conducted in real time, like watching a movie of your insides. He took a long wire that had a slight hook on the end and slowly threaded it up the tube in my arm. I could plainly see the wire as it made its way up into my neck. He then caught the end of the tube with the hooked end and ever so carefully brought the tube back down my neck and rerouted it down the artery toward my heart. That was one freaky experience.

I forgot completely what the nurse had told me about the blue dye they used in my feet. She had said it would eventually come out when I urinated. That night, when I got back to the hotel, I needed to use the little boys' room. As the flow began, I yelled for my best friend, Chris (who came along on that trip), and Deanne to come to the bathroom quick. It was the only light moment that day, as I amazed both Chris and my wife with my display of electric-blue urine.

"Here Comes the Poison"

Deanne was with me as they began the first round of chemo. I could see the drug making its way down the IV, and just as it was about to enter my bloodstream, I blurted out a most insensitive phrase. I looked at Deanne and said, "Here comes the poison." That was not the right thing to say, and she started crying.

As the chemo entered my system, my lower back started hurting, and not long after that, I needed to use the bathroom. The chemo, along with other drip bags, was on a wheeled contraption that looked like a coatrack. As I made my way down the hall toward the bathroom, I thought how odd it was to have to trail this coatrack along with me.

The first two rounds of chemo were delivered in a drip bag; the third was put in a twenty-four-hour infuser, which I took with me back to the hotel. Before I was allowed to leave the hospital, the doctor gave Deanne an emergency number so we could get ahold of him if I had a reaction. The doctor pulled Deanne aside and told her that she needed to keep a close eye on me that evening, saying that I might get sick and probably wouldn't have much of an appetite.

When we got back to the hotel, Deanne asked if I was hungry. I told her I was starving, so she ordered some pizza and Cokes to the room. I ended up eating most of a large pizza myself and surprised her by drinking

Other Artists

In my career I've had the opportunity to collaborate with some outstanding fellow artists. Here's a partial listing:

Dennis Agajanian	Kerry Livgren
Paul and Rita Baloche	Love Song
Margaret Becker	Randy Matthews
Pat Boone	Barry McGuire
The Boone Girls	Don Moen
Carman	Larry Norman
Rick Crawford	Michael and Stormie Omartian
Paul Clark	Jimmy and Carol Owens
Andraé Crouch	Jamie Owens Collins
The Cruise Family	Twila Paris
Mark Farner	The Pat Terry Group
John Fischer	Sandi Patty
Bill and Gloria Gaither	Leslie Phillips
Joseph L. Garlington	LeAnn Rimes
Keith Green	Ricky Skaggs
Steve Green	Randy Stonehill
Jack Hayford	Donna Summers
Steve Holy	John Michael Talbot
Nancy Honeytree	Terry Talbot
Dennis Jernigan	Greg X. Volz
Phil Keaggy	Sheila Walsh
Ron Kenoly	Shannon Wexelberg
Ed Kerr	David Wilkerson
Mylon Le Fevre	

Coke as well. I have never been much of a soft drink fan, but it sounded so good that night. The hospital gave me some drugs for nausea, which I never did need. The only negative reaction I had from the chemo was some minor flulike symptoms and headaches from the Bleo.

We traveled to Houston every three weeks to get another round of drugs. The Bleo was the one I had the most of. I would have a dose of that midweek as well. To save me from having to go to Houston too frequently, they mailed me the Bleo, which I kept in the refrigerator. We'd take it out of the fridge and let it get to room temperature before hooking it up to the long line that had been left in my vein. My friend Steve Ford had a pontoon boat, and whenever I did that particular chemo, he'd pick me up and we'd go bass fishing all day. I found that fishing was the only thing that took my mind off how bad that drug made me feel.

The long line in my arm had to be kept sterile, so it always had high-tech bandages over it. Deanne had taken classes to learn how to clean the long line, flushing it out with saline, and to change the dressing, taking great care to keep that area sterile. The first time I needed the bandage changed, she just looked at me and said, "I can't do it, at least not this time." I didn't blame her; I knew it was emotional for her. So I jumped in the car, drove myself to the hospital in Tyler, and had a nurse there change the dressing. That was the only time Deanne didn't change it for me, and once she started, I noticed right away that she did a better job than the nurse.

M. D. Anderson had developed a new drug, called Neupogin, designed to help the body produce white cells, which were depleted by chemo. The drug was administered through injection in the same fashion that diabetics would inject insulin. Because I'm such a weenie when it comes to giving myself shots, I had Deanne do it for me. She gave me the shots in the back of my arm. I can't believe what a trouper she was through all of it.

During the course of my chemo treatments, I noticed that I wasn't losing all my hair like I thought I would. As a matter of fact, I was the only guy out of thirty in my group who did the same protocol and wasn't totally bald. My hair did get thinner to the point that I ended up cutting off most of my ponytail. One morning I woke up, and as I got out of bed, I looked down where I had been lying, and there were two perfect rows of hair where my legs had been. I knew then for sure how severe the drugs were.

I was fortunate I had to do chemo for only six weeks. The long line was making me crazy, but I learned to deal with it after I talked to a couple of guys who had kept theirs in for a year or more. Still, I can't tell you how great it felt to have that thing removed when I finished my chemo treatments.

Follow-Up

There was still much more that I would have to go through. For the next several years, I had blood work done every month and drove to Houston every three months for a CAT scan. It became a routine that I learned to deal with. I got to the point where I would just make a long day of it and drive back home when I was done—a round trip of nearly five hundred miles.

My test days went something like this. I would get up early in the morning, make the drive to Houston, and have blood work done first thing, so they could make sure my liver was able to handle the iodine. After that, I'd have to wait around for a few hours to get the results. Meanwhile, I would have chest x-rays done. Next, I would head over to where they prepared me for the CAT scan. I would don my hospital robe and get an IV put in my arm so when the time came for the CAT scan, they would be able to inject the iodine.

As I sat in the room awaiting my x-ray, they would make me drink a thousand cc's of barium. I have never drunk latex paint, but I can't imagine that barium is much different. They had some inventive ways of disguising the horrible-tasting goo. One flavor was strawberry, which I hated. Piña colada ended up being the only one I could stomach.

Most of the guys awaiting their turns were older gentlemen who had a much tougher time getting the barium down. So I tried to lighten the mood by saying, "It's happy hour." Then I'd pinch my nose and chug it down. I'd get a big laugh, then watch as a few of them followed my lead. As they slammed their cups down, they'd thank me for showing them the way.

After I had consumed the allotted amount of barium, the medical workers would take me to the room with the CAT scanner, hook up the machine that would inject iodine into my IV, and give me a barium enema. Just before they began the scan, they would inject synthetic iodine into my system. As soon as they injected the stuff, I could smell and taste it.

The CAT scan didn't take long and wasn't hard for me to manage. I just had to follow the automated voice, which told me, "Breathe in. Breathe out. Hold your breath." The machine would take a picture of one part of my body, then it would move me a few inches and repeat the command about holding my breath, take another picture, move me again, and so on, until it had taken pictures of my whole torso. The procedure took about twenty minutes. When I finished, the technicians would unhook me and take me back to the happy-hour room, where they would take the IV out. Then I'd get dressed, hang out at the hospital for another forty-five minutes or so (the barium would do some unusual things to my lower intestinal tract), and when I felt I was ready, make the trip home.

Even though my trips down south became more or less routine, every time I had a test done, I kept thinking, *Is this the day they will find something wrong with me? Will I have to go through all this again? Will I be able to handle it?*

After nearly two years of follow-up, I met a guy while we waited for our CAT scans who told me that after being free from his cancer for seven years, he had just found out that it had returned. Hearing him say that made me so instantly depressed that I was beside myself. I tried to put myself in his shoes and realized what a difficult thing that would be for me to deal with. I prayed for him and myself.

As I write this, it's been ten years to the day since I was diagnosed with cancer. Looking back over that span, I've come to see the Lord's hand on my family and me in obvious and powerful ways. Things happened that I simply didn't understand, such as finding out right before my surgery that the medical insurance company I was with had just filed bankruptcy. That left Deanne and me holding the bill for everything I had to have done. (Even though it cost us plenty, we were fortunate because we lived in the state of Texas and qualified for a program that M. D. Anderson was offering.) Despite such problems, I learned so much through my ordeal that I wouldn't trade it for anything in the world.

Cancer's Gifts

One day, while I was going through chemo, my six-year-old daughter Morgan came up to me and asked if I was going to die.

All I could do was look her straight in the eyes and say, "I don't know."

I didn't expect the response I got. She looked at me and said, "Okay," then ran off to play with her friends.

Kids are funny. Sometimes all they want is an answer.

My answer to my daughter was truthful. I really didn't know whether I would live or die from the cancer. And that required me to stop and think about my faith in God. I trusted that God would do well for me, but what if He decided not to heal me? Would I still trust Him? I came to the place where I committed to trust Him even if He should slay me (see Job 13:15). How many of us can truly say that?

For years I had a warped perspective of God as a father figure. I think it stemmed from losing both parents at such an early age. I knew God loved me, but I had a tendency to view that love more as a generic love, one that God has for everyone. I found it difficult to see God as someone who thought about *my* needs or loved *me* in a deeply personal way.

During and after my ordeal with cancer, the Lord began to show me in big and small ways that I was truly on His mind and that He was indeed concerned with those things that concerned me. I learned to see the father heart of God for the first time, and I began to see myself as His son. Of all the lessons I learned, that—by far—was the greatest.

I also learned who my true friends were. There were people in my life who I had thought would always be there for me, but when they got word that I was dealing with cancer, they were nowhere to be found. Others I wouldn't have counted on were there with unbelievable support.

Looking back from where I am today, I don't blame those who disappeared; it can be a hard thing just to be there for someone. We feel we need to have something profound to say, and when we don't, it's easier to avoid the situation.

I have often been reminded of the story of Job. When Job's friends showed up, they sat with him for seven days and seven nights before one word was spoken. Why? Because "they saw how great his suffering was" (Job 2:13). Sometimes what we need most is for our friends to merely sit with us.

Why We Follow God

Many years ago, the sister of our pastor had cancer, and all the church prayed for her and believed for her healing. One night, during a service, we set aside time to pray for her. I felt a stirring in my spirit and believed the

Lord was going to touch her for healing. Well, she died. For a long time I questioned that. I couldn't understand why God didn't touch this wonderful daughter of His for healing. This experience reinforced for me the idea that God's ways are not my ways, but it also caused me for many years not to give my heart to prayer like I should.

Now, I don't want to leave you with the impression that I believe God doesn't heal people today. I know better from firsthand experience. I've prayed for plenty of people and watched God's hand move. It's just that I get tired of Christians thinking they have answers for everything we face in life. We all must face God's sovereignty.

I look at it like this: We're all terminal. We've all got a certain number of years appointed to us, and that's it. It's what we do with those years that matters. The Lord's decision to heal someone (or not) should not be the reason we follow Him (or not). We just have to be obedient to what God has for us in however many years He gives us on this earth. Whether I live or die, it is all for Christ—that, to me, is what is important. Everything good will come out of that.

As it turned out, I lived through my cancer. In a way, as my cancer treatments were coming to an end, I was beginning the second half of my life. I had survived; what did God have for me now?

15

My Redeemer

You might think, after I had gone through successful cancer surgery and follow-up chemotherapy—with every appearance of having eliminated the illness from my body—I would have been thrilled, upbeat, and looking toward the future.

Instead a dark cloud rose on my horizon.

Some months after finishing chemo, I began to recognize signs of depression in me. Listlessness and discouragement settled in. Although my body had been healed, I guess my mind and spirit were still dealing with fallout from my ordeal.

When I'd gone through the depression shortly after Second Chapter ended, I just gritted my teeth and rode it out. This time, though, I honestly didn't think I could face that pit again. So I decided to see a doctor and find out whether there was something he could do to stop the downward spiral of melancholy.

During my appointment, the doctor grilled me with a bunch of psychological questions. When he'd finished with me, he recommended that I start taking the antidepressant Prozac.

I wasn't thrilled with the idea of taking a mood-altering drug. It seemed that everybody had started taking this new drug, and I wasn't keen to jump on the bandwagon. I shared my feelings with the doctor, but he assured me that I would be better off taking it. And to be honest, I was so desperate that I would have tried just about anything to avoid going through severe depression again.

The drug did stop my depression from getting worse, but it also made me not care about anything. I became a spineless, passive, no-opinion-about-anything kind of guy. While I was taking the drug, I felt as if, assuming my house had caught fire with me and all my family in it, I would have calmly said to my wife, "Get the kids. Grab what you don't want to see get burned. I'll make my way out to the front yard and meet up with you." I felt like I'd had a frontal lobotomy. I didn't give a rip about anything.

At the same time—and I don't know if this was more due to the depression or to the antidepressant—it seemed as if God had lost my address. When I prayed, I felt like my words were bouncing off the walls and falling to the floor. For a guy who had often had an intimate experience of God, this was one of the hardest things to take.

I stayed on the drug for only a few months. I just couldn't stand how it made me feel. But I knew my problems were not yet fully resolved. So I decided to try a little therapy of my own: I would take my problems straight to God. It might have seemed like He had lost my address, but in my head, if not in my heart, I knew He was still there and cared for me.

I began getting up early and going immediately up to my office, where I would start writing. I would simply let my emotions go and say on paper whatever I felt. Some of what I wrote ended up becoming letters to God. I figured that God didn't suffer from an inferiority complex, and nothing I could say was going to catch Him off guard.

One morning, while I was preparing to write down more of my feelings, I decided I was going to write, in a poetic form, the things I believed about God. It was like taking all the great stuff I'd learned over the years—

all the wonderful sermons I'd heard and the powerful things I'd read—and putting all of it aside in order to ask myself the question "What do I really believe to be true of God?" It was a melting away of what I had *heard* to be true, and what I had *assumed* to be true, so that I could get down to the nuts and bolts of my actual faith.

The words I wrote that morning were intended to be only another attempt to air out my spiritual laundry, but God had other things in mind.

Songs from God—Through Annie

After I came out of my depression, which ended as quickly as it began, I showed my sister Annie what I had written about my beliefs of God. I thought that she, of all people, would appreciate the honesty of what I'd said.

After Annie read my letter, she looked at me and said, "Can I take these words home with me? I'd like to see if I get any music for it."

I told Annie, "I have no intention of my letter ever becoming a song." But I could tell she wanted to take a stab at putting music to it.

She called me the next day and told me, "I finished the song. Would you like to come over and hear it?"

I had mixed emotions about her endeavors, simply because I wasn't sure I could handle hearing something so personal of mine being put to music. But of course I said I would listen. And her song was great; it really captured what I had been feeling. Still, my feelings about the personal nature of my letter hadn't changed.

"You did a great job with the song, but I don't think I can ever sing it," I told Annie.

Looking back, it's obvious to me that God wanted the simple message of that song to be heard. I did end up recording the song—"To the King"—

one of the most popular songs I've ever done. That song was God's way of getting me to look at what I'd been through in a different light. Furthermore, it started a stirring in my heart, a desire to produce an album centered on my experiences with cancer. It would be a CD that would offer hope to those who had gone through, or who were going through, struggles that seemed bigger than they were. It would be something that might give hope to those who felt disillusioned in their walk with God.

A few months after Annie wrote the music for "To the King," she called and said, "The Lord has given me a song that you are supposed to sing."

I tried to get more information out of her on the phone, but she told me, "You need to come by my place so I can sing it to you."

After I arrived, we went to her studio and she began explaining something to me: "I had a really hard time when you were going through your bout with cancer," she said. "I had difficulties coming to grips with your suffering. But now that some time has passed, I feel I am at a place to hear from the Lord concerning you."

She went on to tell me, "One morning I was sitting at my piano, and the Lord gave me a glimpse of what it must have been like for you to go through all the procedures. As I contemplated your ordeal, I received a song from the Lord about your struggles. It is a song you are supposed to sing."

At this point I looked at her and skeptically asked, "Annie, why on earth would the Lord give *you* a song about *my* ordeal? You write songs and I write songs. Why would God give that song to you and not to me?"

She looked up from her piano and said, "Sometimes the things that are deep down inside us, those things that God wants to use the most, require someone to come alongside and help pull them out."

I decided I would hold my tongue and reserve judgment until I heard what the Lord had given her.

As she began the song, I knew instantly that the Holy Spirit was all over what she was playing. I had goose bumps up and down my body. In her lyrics I could feel every bit of the emotion I had been through. It's a mystery to me how she did it, but she really hit the nail on the head about my feelings. When she finished singing, my eyes were full of tears. I had no doubt that the Lord had given her a view into my experience.

My Redeemer

With the song "To the King" and the new song Annie had written, "God Almighty," the possibility of a new CD went from being a good idea to something I felt commanded by God to do. I started selecting other songs that I felt would embody the spirit of what I wanted to convey. Among these were tunes I had recently been introduced to while rehearsing for Promise Keepers. They included the songs "I See the Lord," by Chris Falson, and another song I fell in love with called "Knowing You," by Graham Kendrick.

When the project was finally finished, I called it *My Redeemer*, which was the title of one of the songs in the collection—one my sister Annie had written a few years earlier.

As I began to pursue the normal avenues to get this CD made, I came up against some unexpected resistance. Even though I did the best I could to explain this new musical direction to executives from the record label I was with at the time, they were less than encouraging. They thought I should put this new music off for a while and pursue the musical direction I had already established. But I felt so strongly about doing this new CD that after going back and forth with folks from my label and coming to an impasse, I ended up leaving them.

Deanne and I decided that if this new CD was a "God thing," we'd pursue any avenue we could. Not seeing any other way to get it done, we took out a second mortgage on our house to pay for the production. It's one of the few times in my life I felt strongly enough about a project to risk everything to see it happen.

It was interesting to watch the production of this new CD come together. I did half the production in Los Angeles and the other half with my longtime friends at Rosewood Studios in Tyler, Texas.

I started the process with my good friend Smitty Price, who has a small overdub studio in his house in the Los Angeles area. As we worked out the basic arrangements of the tunes, I mentioned I wanted to re-record something I'd originally done in 1977 on a live Second Chapter album called *How the West Was One.* The song was called "Psalm 61," and originally it had been done with just my vocal accompanied by piano. I had never felt that the full potential of the tune had been realized. Now I felt that the Lord wanted to use that song for a new generation.

Worship Music

Before the release of *My Redeemer,* I played several of the songs for friends.

I had Chris Snell, my best friend, listen to the entire disc at my house. I respected his opinion and wanted to know what he would think of it. As I played it, he sat there quietly, never saying a word, even after the music ended. He simply remained silent.

Then, as I worried that he might not have liked what he heard, he finally turned to me and said, "Matt, I'm not just saying this because we're good friends, but that's the best worship CD I've ever heard."

As we began working on "Psalm 61," I had no concrete sense of what direction to take. Toying with different ideas, we started down a musical road that blew us both away. At one point Smitty was sitting with his back toward me, loading our new ideas into his computer, when the spirit of true worship filled the room. The Holy Spirit showed up so strongly that we both stopped at the same instant. Smitty slowly turned around, looked up at me, and in a hushed tone said, "Man, do you feel that?" I knew in that holy moment that the Lord had big plans for the song. We actually stopped and worshiped for a while. But it wasn't until I'd been doing "Psalm 61" live for a few months that the Lord revealed to me that it was to be used for deliverance.

I was in the Midwest doing a concert one night and was getting ready to introduce the song, when suddenly I felt I needed to say something

At first I didn't know how to take his comment. Worship music was something that was gaining in popularity at the time, and I didn't want this piece of music—something I'd poured so much of my heart into—viewed as simply another worship album. I told him so.

"No," he said, clarifying, "I've never heard music that made me want to worship more. As I listened, I felt that it was allowing me to worship."

A few days later I dropped off a copy for another friend, Burt. He had been suffering for some time with hepatitis, and I thought it might minister to him. I talked with him a few days later, and he said, "From the moment the music began until it was finished, all I could do was lie facedown in front of my stereo and weep."

special to the people gathered there: "I want you to think about something that's keeping you from being as close to the Lord as you'd like to be," I started. "It could be a relationship; it could be financial problems; it could be self-doubt—whatever issue in your life is keeping you from just diving in and giving yourself to the Lord.

"This song is a cry of David's heart. He was surrounded by armies, and although he had a citadel, he was always vulnerable in his prayers. You would think that someone who had that much security would be more bold, but he was always crying out, 'O God, help me through this. People are trying to kill me.'

"So I'm going to sing this song over you as a prayer, because that's what it is. And whatever that thing is that's keeping you from the Lord, figuratively put it in your hands and offer it to Him tonight."

Later, I got a couple of letters from people who were in the crowd that night, telling me how powerful it was for them. One woman wrote that while I was singing the song, she could see something that looked like electric snowflakes falling upon all the people who were open to having God move in their lives. She could also see things in their hands dissolving—just going away, vanishing.

That's exactly what I was feeling when I sang "Psalm 61" that night.

For the first year, Deanne and I sold *My Redeemer* from our house. We filled orders from a Web site, then we hired a friend of ours to do the radio tracking (making follow-up calls to radio stations to see how often they are playing the song). Two number one songs came from that project ("To the King" and "Drink Deep"). Many in the Christian music industry were amazed that we could have such success with an independent record. The CD became what the industry calls an evergreen project, meaning that it sold as well after two years as it did when it was first released.

Looking back, it's obvious that God wanted that CD produced, and it never ceases to amaze me how many people God still touches with it. I wish I had kept all the letters from people who shared stories of the amazing things that happened to them when they listened. Some people would hear one of the songs on the radio, and they'd have to pull off the freeway because they couldn't see through the tears.

For the first five or six years after completing that music, I performed the songs from that CD all over America. I can't recall one time when the Lord didn't touch someone in a powerful way. Even though I've recorded a new CD since then, called *Even Now,* and had incredible results with it as well, there still is something special about the anointing on the *My Redeemer* project.

Even Now

The CD *Even Now* was a natural next step after *My Redeemer.* Whereas *My Redeemer* dealt with issues directly related to my ordeal with cancer, *Even Now* addressed issues more related to walking out a life with Christ in a real, day-to-day way.

The song "Even Now" came about after a conversation I had with a good friend of mine, Kurt Heineke. Kurt produces much of the music for Big Idea, the company that creates the VeggieTales series. Kurt was telling me about their latest venture, a full-length movie based on the story of Jonah. After our conversation, I was curious to read that story in the Bible through a fresh pair of glasses, so to speak. As I read the familiar story, I was struck for the first time with the idea of sin's power not only to affect me but also, if left unchecked, to have far-reaching consequences for those within my circle of influence.

When I started writing the lyrics to "Even Now," I had no idea what the song was about; I just started writing down some lines that I felt painted a portrait of God's unconditional love for His children. As I got most of the way through the first verse, though, I began to realize that the song was really about God's heart toward Jonah while he was yet in the belly of the fish. I could almost hear the Lord speaking to Jonah's heart, comforting him during a time when I'm sure Jonah felt that God was far from him. I saw a picture of all of us when we feel God has abandoned us, left us to figure out our own way through life's seemingly impossible circumstances. I thought about my own life, all the times when I felt that God had turned a deaf ear to my cries. In hindsight, I could see that even in the worst of those times, the hand of the Father had held my hand when I had no strength of my own to carry on.

That song became a great reminder of God's unfailing love, not only for me personally, but for many others who have heard it as well. What a privilege it is for me, as a singer and songwriter, to serve as a conduit for God's ministry to those He loves.

16

Rocky Mountain Musician

For nearly a year after finishing chemo, I didn't do many live performances. I just wasn't physically up to the challenges of life on the road.

In 1995, around the time I was considering the project that would become *My Redeemer*, I still didn't have a handle on what I wanted to do long term.

As I was thinking of different avenues, I had several conversations with my good friend, Buddy Owens, who was then working with Promise Keepers, the group that puts on conferences for men. In the mid-1990s Promise Keepers was experiencing a meteoric rise in popularity and publicity. I suggested to Buddy that maybe I should be involved with Promise Keepers, but I wasn't sure in what capacity.

Buddy affirmed what I was saying and told me I needed to come to the event they were putting on in Denver, Colorado. I explained to him that I would love more than anything to be there, but since I was living in Texas and low on funds, I couldn't afford to hop on a plane and show up. He graciously sent me an airline ticket.

It was refreshing for me to be around so many strong Christian men, and Buddy demanded nothing more of me than to hang out with him and get a feel for what the Lord was doing through Promise Keepers. The event was at the old Mile High Stadium, and the weekend contributed in a big way to my spiritual and emotional healing.

There was one moment in particular that I will never forget. I had spent much of the weekend backstage, keeping an eye on what was going on while trying my best to stay out of people's hair. So I decided I needed to get out into the crowd and get a better feel for the spiritual atmosphere in the stadium. As I made my way out onto the field, I positioned myself in the dead center of the stadium, not far from the sound engineer. I don't know how many people Mile High seated, but it was full. I wasn't in my position long before the worship team led the men in the old hymn "A Mighty Fortress."

As the men began singing, I was overwhelmed by the sheer power of their voices proclaiming the doctrinal truths of that song. I tried my best to join in, but every time I did so, my throat would choke off. Finally I felt the Lord saying to me, *Son, don't sing. Let Me minister to you.* All I could do was weep as the sound made by thousands of male voices washed over me.

From that moment, I knew I wanted to be involved with Promise Keepers in any way I could.

As it turned out, my friend Buddy was in charge of putting the worship teams together for the 1996 season. He called me and asked if I wanted a spot on one of the four teams being put together. I said of course I would and requested assignment to the team headed up by my friend Smitty Price.

I was involved in eleven Promise Keepers events in 1996, all of which were held in large football stadiums. The first event I sang at was in the Oakland Raiders stadium. I've sung to some large crowds before, but nothing prepared me for the energy that so many men could generate. When we started off a song, the crowd of men erupted into singing. The feeling I had instantly reminded me of the "Mighty Fortress" experience a year earlier in Denver. I started to choke-up in the same way but pressed through and kept on singing. If anything, my feelings were even more intense this time because I was onstage helping lead the worship.

You might think that after seven or eight events like that, the feeling would diminish, but it never did. Every time we took the stage to sing and lead worship, we felt the overwhelming presence of God.

We did have some fun, too.

At one event Smitty Price, who was the band director, and I thought it would be interesting if we had all the singers play instruments and all the players take the mikes and sing. We ran the idea by the stage manager, who wasn't thrilled with the idea, but he let us go ahead and try it for one song. As we decided which singer would play which instrument (we wanted it to at least sound decent), Smitty suggested that I be the drummer. I had jammed with him before, and he knew I had a knack for playing the drums. Once we got the list of players figured out, we decided on a song— a simple number with a strong rock beat, so it was pretty hard to screw up.

When it came time for us to take the stage, the worship leader, Joseph Garlington, announced to the crowd that we were going to change things up a little. Even though we had worked out exactly who was going to do what, Joseph made it sound like it was an idea that had just popped into his head. He began calling out the names of different singers and assigning them to the instruments he wanted them to play. When he got to me, he said, "Matthew Ward, I want you playing drums." So I left my microphone and got situated behind the drum set. We could tell by the audience reaction that, if nothing else, we were going to have a little fun.

Once everyone was in place, it was time to start the tune. Part of my job was to count off the intro to the song. I took a second to get the tune in my head, and with what I felt to be an appropriate tempo in mind, I raised the drumsticks over my head and in true rock fashion clicked them together as I yelled out, "One, two, three…"

Even though I loved to play drums, I had never played them in public before. Yet here I was onstage, concentrating on doing a good job, when it hit me that I was playing drums in a band to more than fifty thousand people. I really wanted to be half decent.

As the song got under way, I happened to look up—and there, on the Jumbotron, was a close-up of my face. That was the weirdest feeling I've ever had onstage, seeing my face plastered on a giant screen while doing something I had never done before. I had to look away, because I knew that if I kept looking, I'd mess up for sure.

When we finished with our song, we walked offstage and talked about how it came off. I thought we had done pretty well, but the stage coordinator didn't share my conviction. That was the last time we were allowed to do that.

Music Maker

My experience with Promise Keepers in 1996 was one of the most fulfilling times of my life. It was a wonderful feeling working with such great people, being part of something that led so many men in the power of worship. It led me in a return to the power of worship as well.

Another thing Promise Keepers did for me was to renew my passion for music ministry. I knew now that I wanted to continue serving the Lord and His people through the gift of music He had given me. I was still full of musical ideas, and my musical judgment had matured to a point where I believed I had something important to offer.

Meanwhile, as my stint with Promise Keepers was coming to an end, I grew increasingly discontented with living in Texas. I'd arrive back in Lindale after Promise Keepers events or other gigs and not feel like I was coming home. It was the weirdest thing. After all, I'd lived in that area for the better part of two decades. But I started discussing a move with Deanne, and she was open to that idea.

Nellie and Annie and their husbands had already moved to different parts of Colorado—Nellie to the Front Range and Annie to the western mountain region. Visiting them, as well as doing projects for Colorado-based ministries like Focus on the Family and Compassion International, showed me how beautiful Colorado really is. Not to mention how much better the climate is than in Texas! In 1998 Deanne and I and our three girls moved into a home near Nellie's.

After settling in Colorado, I continued—and even expanded—the musical activities I had been doing in Texas after Second Chapter of Acts disbanded. My career has been a mix of songwriting, recording my own CDs, singing live as a solo act or with other performers, providing background vocals, producing CDs for others, recording commercial jingles, and even doing voice-overs for animated movie characters. I love every part of this mix; each is challenging and rewarding in its own way.

One day I got a call from my engineering friend Greg Hunt in Tyler, Texas, saying he was working with a new artist, a young lady he felt might have a real chance in the country music industry. He wanted to know if I'd consider singing backgrounds on her project.

"Of course," I told him.

He then went on to ask if I'd be on my best behavior. The reason for this was that, more times than not, Greg and I would cut up in the studio. But this time he didn't want to jeopardize his chances with this new artist, who was barely a teenager.

After I assured him that I'd be a perfect gentleman, he told me what time to show up for the session.

I met this teenager, LeAnn Rimes, in the foyer of the studio a few minutes before the session began. In that first brief conversation I sensed this
young lady acted older than her years. As the other singers showed up, we
congregated in the studio to do microphone level checks.

I was thrown back in time as I relived my first studio experience, when
I had recorded "Jesus Is" on the day before my thirteenth birthday. I realized that LeAnn was about the same age as I was when I began my recording career. The first song we worked on was "Blue," which had a retro
country feel. I found out during the session that the song was originally
written for Patsy Cline, but she'd died in a plane crash before she could
record it. I took a liking to the song right away, and for me it was refreshing to hear a young artist singing a song with such strong country roots.

After LeAnn's CD *Blue* hit the market, it didn't take long for the title
song to shoot up through the charts to the number one position.

When you're working on a project, you never know how it will do on
the radio. LeAnn's "Blue" (1996) was not the only song I sang backgrounds
on and that made it to number one. I also did background on Donna Summers's "She Works Hard for the Money" (1983) and the Steve Holy country tune "Good Morning, Beautiful" (2002).

Several times I have been singing along with a song I'm hearing on the
radio and suddenly realized that I'm one of the background singers. It's a
strange feeling to be listening to yourself, knowing that millions of people
are hearing you sing but no one knows it's you back there.

Actually, I like the idea of making a musical contribution without
being in the limelight. I can do that, too, while producing albums for
others. I've long had a gift for seeing and achieving the potential in a song.
That's what I love about producing music. Of course, the budget might
prevent me from doing all I might want—I can't necessarily afford to rent

the London Philharmonic—so I have to figure out how to make the music good with what's available.

At one time I helped with a record for Rick Crawford, who used to play bass for Dallas Holm. Live Oak, his label, hired me to produce it. The way I worked with Rick illustrates how I usually like to produce.

First I said to Rick, "Let me hear all the songs you've got—anything you might want to stick on this record."

So he gave me a rough cassette of twenty songs with just him playing. That's all I had to go by. But still, even with a song in a raw state like that, I would think, *Well, it would be cool to do it this way.* I would hear a guitar doing this or the drums doing that. Then I would talk to Rick about what I was hearing in my head, and we would start putting a plan together to get musicians to do what we wanted on the recording.

Piece by piece, the record came together. I love that feeling of building up something musically that barely existed as a set of ideas before.

Minister with Music

I still perform my own music fairly frequently at churches and other venues. Most recently, I have begun singing for a series of pastors' conferences put on by my old friend Gary Wilkerson, son of David Wilkerson.

These days, when I present a concert, I usually do songs from either *My Redeemer* or *Even Now.* I rarely mix the two. In part that's because I generally sing to tracks prerecorded in the studio, and those two projects were recorded differently and don't sound the same. But another part of it has to do with the contexts of those two projects. *My Redeemer* is related to my cancer experience, while *Even Now* has a different orientation entirely.

Normally, people like to hear where songs came from, what I was going

My Wife the Tomato

Over the last few years, Deanne and I have struck up a friendship with Kurt Heinecke, the music producer for the VeggieTales children's videos. After our many conversations with Kurt, he recognized Deanne's ability for organization and promotion of musical concepts. So when VeggieTales was preparing to release *King George and the Ducky*, Kurt asked Deanne if she would spearhead a premier at the church we were attending at the time—the largest church in Colorado Springs.

We knew putting on an event like this would be a considerable amount of work, but we had a feeling it could also be tons of fun. As the day approached for the premier, we had most details covered but were still working on getting Bob the Tomato and Larry the Cucumber to the event. It was my understanding that when VeggieTales puts on a premiere, only one of the star veggies makes an appearance. But Deanne never does anything halfway, and she held out for both.

Larry's and Bob's costumes are complex, each costing thousands of dollars. They're shipped separately in their own hard-sided cases and come complete with instructions. Each has a heavy battery pack that the person inside the suit straps on. These batteries (which work for about twenty minutes) power the internal fans that keep Bob and Larry inflated.

Just before showing the video, we brought Bob and Larry onto the stage, and all the kids—twenty-five hundred of them—went crazy. After the video ended, we had a time when the kids could meet and greet the vegetables.

However, for some reason, the person inside the Bob costume was unable to stay for the meet-and-greet. Deanne happened to fit the height requirements for Bob, so she said she'd give it a try. It was hilarious watching her struggle to get into the heavy and cumbersome outfit.

Once Deanne was good to go, we led her into the main sanctuary. She was still getting used to the bulky tomato suit when out of nowhere a little kid who couldn't contain his excitement decided to wrap himself around Bob the Tomato's legs. Deanne nearly crushed the tyke because she had limited vision while wearing the suit.

After she entertained the kids for twenty-five minutes or so, we noticed that the tomato was withering. The batteries were about to die. It was more than a little humorous to watch Deanne trying to race back to the dressing room before the tomato deflated completely. I could imagine how hard it would be to explain to the kiddies that Bob was feeling a bit flat.

We were able to whisk Bob into the dressing room just before he became grotesquely deformed. They quickly switched batteries, and after Bob had reinflated, he was brought back to a smaller room where the meet-and-greet continued.

I waited in line with the rest of the kids to have my family's picture taken with Bob and Larry. I framed that picture, and it sits in my living room. When friends see it and ask, "Where's Deanne?" I always get a kick out of telling them, "She's in the tomato."

through when I wrote them, and so I try to get into that in my concerts. I'll introduce each song and give a synopsis of what was happening when I wrote it. Or maybe a song will remind me of another incident that happened to me. I don't plan too much what I'm going to say; instead, I fly by the seat of my pants. I have to admit, sometimes that works and sometimes it doesn't. Occasionally I'll tell people, "My train doesn't have a caboose— you can come along for the ride or not."

Regardless of what songs I'm singing, I try to fit my ministry to the needs of the people in front of me. And so, when I get to a church where I'm going to perform, I attempt to get a feel for what the church is all about, what it's going through, what the pastor and worship team are like. Since I usually sing a few songs in a Sunday morning worship service, with a full concert to follow in the evening, I can usually pick up quite a bit about the church before my own concert. Then I tailor the evening to the church's needs.

When I have time to prepare, I get serious about it and pray, *Lord, show me what You want for this group. I'm not here by accident.* And sometimes the Lord starts showing me things—maybe about the leadership of the church, maybe about where the church is hurting, maybe even areas where I can encourage them in what they are doing well.

Sometimes I get incredibly specific or powerful impressions from the Lord. Sometimes I'll be in the middle of a song and I can hardly get through it because I start sensing some need. I get choked up to the point where I can barely sing. In between songs, I'll give the people a word from the Lord.

For example, I have said, "You have been here for a few years, and you want to do things in the community, but for some reason those things haven't happened yet. But God has placed you here as a beacon in your community. God is going to do things through you." I think saying such things helps people be more bold in following the Lord. And often I get letters from people later telling me that what I foretold actually came to pass.

My role model in all of this is my sister Annie. She believes that music is a living entity and that God uses it in different ways in different lives at different times. And I've seen that to be true. So my attitude is this: if God wants to speak, let Him speak.

In the spring of 1997, I was in Hawaii at New Hope Christian Fellowship, a Foursquare church where the pastor is Wayne Cordeiro. While I was singing on a Sunday morning, I suddenly received a strong impression that God wanted to heal the physical illness of someone in the congregation. So I stopped and told the listeners, "I feel like the power of God is here to heal, to touch your body if you have physical problems. If you need me to pray for you, seek me out later."

After the service, a young woman came up and started explaining that she had lupus and was struggling physically. As this soft-spoken woman told me her story, I felt the Lord saying to me, *I want you to pray for her healing.*

I said to the woman, "I believe that God is going to heal you. I'm going to pray for you, and God is going to heal you." I didn't give myself an out, like saying that God would use the hands of the doctors or adding "if it's His will." No, I just went for it. I realize that sometimes God chooses to heal and sometimes He doesn't, but on this occasion I was sure He wanted to heal the woman.

"Do you believe in the healing power of God?" I asked her.

"Yes, I do."

"Even if you didn't," I told her, "God is still going to heal you right now."

She just nodded. I don't know what she was thinking.

Then I prayed for her. I don't remember the words I used, but I felt the unction of the Holy Spirit, and it was powerful.

I went back to the church a year or two later, and a woman came up to me. She looked familiar. I asked her, "Are you the lady I prayed with to be healed of lupus?"

"Yes."

"What happened?"

"I went to the doctor and it was gone."

Christian Classics

In 1988, after Second Chapter did what I called the cruise from hell, I thought I'd never go on a cruise again. Then fifteen years later, in 2003, I was asked to be involved in some concerts on a cruise to Alaska. In recent years I had been to Alaska on several occasions doing solo concerts, mostly in the Kenai area, and I had fallen in love with Alaska. So when the opportunity to do a cruise to Alaska came up, I thought it might be worth a try.

The cruise's theme was based on a Christian classics idea—getting some of the older Christian artists together and doing concerts for people who might be interested in hearing pioneers of contemporary Christian music. I took my oldest daughter, Megin, with me. We had a great time, which helped change my mind about cruises in general.

In June of 2005 I was asked to do another cruise to Alaska, based on the same theme. Buck suggested that Annie (who was another artist invited on the cruise) and I should do a minitour that would begin a few days before the cruise and end with a few dates afterward. I had done a few concerts with Annie over the years since Second Chapter concluded, so I thought this would be fun.

Since the years of Second Chapter, Annie had been doing concerts by singing along with prerecorded tracks, and I had adopted a similar mode of performing. Buck had all the old master recordings of Second Chapter's stuff, and his idea was to get those old tapes and make rough mixes, minus some of the lead vocals, so we'd have something to sing to. He had to take the old tapes and bake them in an oven at a very low temperature so the backing wouldn't come off when run through the tape machines.

After Buck had transferred the analog tapes to a digital format, I went to Buck and Annie's house, where they have their studio, and we listened to the different songs, deciding which tunes might work. We spent the better part of a day listening to different songs, keeping some and eliminating others, and then spent a couple more days rehearsing the songs we wanted to do.

We traveled to the West Coast and began our minitour. We had a prearranged pattern for our concerts. Annie would start out the concert by doing her set, then I'd come out and do mine. After we took a short intermission, Annie and I would come out together and finish the night by doing all Second Chapter tunes. It was a blast.

After doing the first set of concerts, it was time for the cruise. Deanne flew into Seattle to join us. We had traveled together in Alaska before, mixing concerts with fishing trips, and she had really enjoyed it. But that had been traveling by car. Now we were talking about spending days on a ship. She had avoided ships ever since the cruise from hell because of her seasickness. But our doctor suggested we try the newest generation motion sickness patch, and in fact, other than making Deanne sleep a lot, it seemed to do the trick.

I really wanted Deanne to go on this cruise. I had a feeling she would love the quaint port towns that the ship would visit, not to mention all the breathtaking scenery. In Alaskan waters you never know when you're going to see a whale breach or catch a close-up view of a bald eagle skimming the water in search of its next meal.

Then there are the glaciers. To me, that's almost worth the trip right there—pulling into Glacier Bay, getting as close to the wall of ice as the captain deems safe (never close enough for me), then standing and watching as the gigantic ship is brought to a stop. The engines are slowed to a very quiet level, allowing us to hear the glaciers making all the noises they're famous for.

On this cruise we stood on deck and listened with our cameras in hand, waiting for the unmistakable *crack* as the icebergs caved into the ocean. The trick was trying to catch the icebergs with our camera as they slid down the face of the glacier and before they slammed into the ocean below. If we waited for the *crack,* it was usually too late to get a great shot before the berg hit the water. I got pretty good at looking at the face of the glacier and figuring out what area was most likely to send the next berg crashing down.

After the cruise, Annie and I completed our short tour. In some ways these concerts didn't surprise me, but in other ways they did. As expected, the response was enthusiastic from the old die-hard Second Chapter fans. Most of their reactions hinged on reliving their experiences with the group. They went something like this: "I asked my girlfriend to marry me after your concert." "I got saved at one of your concerts." "I couldn't afford to take my girlfriend out on a date. I'm so glad you guys didn't charge for us to come." (I think those were the people who kept our offering averages so low!)

There were some who came up to us after we sang, and we could see in their eyes that the group had meant more than just a cheap date. The Lord had met them, not just that night, but for years as they would listen to the albums we put out.

I've heard so many comments over the years begin with "I first saw you guys in…" or "I heard you guys when you came to…" that, when I hear such things, sometimes it's all I can do not to let my eyes glaze over. I fight to keep their voices from turning into something akin to the adult voices you hear in a Charlie Brown cartoon—*"Gwaa gwaa gwahhh…gwah gwah gwah gwahhhhh."* The thing that saves me is, years ago, someone told me that even though I may have heard the same rhetoric over and over again, it's the first time that particular person has shared it with me. Realizing this has helped me keep my ears and heart attentive to what they are telling me and to give weight to their stories.

The same mentality also helped keep fresh the songs we sang over and over again.

What did surprise me about the concerts before and after the cruise was the number of children being introduced to our music by their friends or family. I could tell when I spoke with these kids that they genuinely enjoyed the music, that they hadn't just been hauled to the concerts and told by their parents to say this or that to us out of politeness. It's really true how music can carry over to different generations. Good music has a way of transcending time and age; it can be enjoyed by young and old alike, now and in the future.

Well, I may have aged into the Christian classics category, but I'm thankful that I'm still writing, still singing, still recording, still producing, still touching others and being touched by them in turn. Annie was right— music is a living entity that God goes on using as He sees fit. How good He is to keep using the gift of music He gave me, year in and year out, to return glory to Himself.

17

Musing on Music

Music has the ability to do what no other form of art can do—grab people by the soul and shake them up. It also has a way of staying in the memory like nothing else—more so than paintings or sculptures, even though those art forms affect us in powerful ways too.

Music, much like scent, has the power to trigger my memory far more than things I have only seen. When I hear a song from the past, I'm taken back to the moment when I first heard that song; I can remember what I was doing, thinking, and feeling at the time.

Music gets inside and goes to work on us. That's music's power and music's potential.

I'll always love music. More than anything else, my musical ability is what God has given me to touch people's lives for His sake. Using music, I can express the creative and redemptive aspects of God in a way that is impossible for me with any other medium. It should be no surprise, then, that I am passionate about this art form—about making, enjoying, and sharing music with others.

It's safe to say I have an unusual perspective when it comes to the music scene. Though I believe I'm nowhere nearly done with music, I want to share a few things I've learned during my first thirty-five years of involvement with music. First of all, I'd like to address those who feel they should be involved in Christian music.

Called to Music Ministry

Many, many times after concerts, I'm approached by people who say, "I feel like I'm supposed to be doing music for the Lord" or "How can I get involved in Christian music?"

I always try and find out right away why people want to get involved in Christian music. The way I see it, music ministry is something that requires a call from the Lord. Even when people have the musical gifting that would allow them to perform Christian songs, that doesn't necessarily mean they should do it—not if they haven't been called to that kind of service by God.

When people ask me how to get into Christian music, I ask them a couple of basic questions about how they see God using them. I first heard Buck ask people these questions, and I have used variations of them over the years to help people define what their ministry role, if any, might be.

First, I ask, "Do you want to entertain or to minister?" In asking this, I'm not implying that ministry can't be entertaining; I'm just trying to establish a sense of the other person's overall thinking. Still, it's one thing to be an entertainer and another to bring true ministry in the form of music.

If all you want to do is entertain, then the weight of responsibility is greatly reduced. It doesn't require an anointing from God simply to tickle the ears. However, if one's goals are to reach the hearts of people and see the power of God fall upon an audience, that requires a lot more from the individual who takes the platform.

Second, I ask, "Do you want to get involved in music because it's something you think you'd be good at or because it's something that's tugging at your heart?" I'm wondering, would they be content with singing in their church for a few people, or do they feel the need to be out in front of a lot of people? In other words, would they be fulfilled if the Lord said to them, "My child, what I have for you is to sing worship to Me in a small church in Kansas all your days"? Or would that prospect make them more than a little discontented? Do they feel the need to impress people with their gift, or are they willing to die to what they think might be best for them and simply worship?

I can tell right away by their responses whether they have given the question of surrender to God's will more than a passing thought.

When I'm asked how to break into the music scene, what I tell them often is not what they want to hear. I could give them a stock answer I've heard over the years: "You need to do a demo of your music and submit it to different record labels." Maybe that's not a bad idea, but what I've discovered is that most record executives don't have the time or the inclination to listen to a tape by an unknown artist.

What I tell people (and I'm sure to many it sounds naive) is that if they seek the Lord with their talents and put Him first in their desires, He will make a way for them.

I say all this from a perspective of personal experience. As I've said before, having a platform in music was never a goal that my sisters or I set for ourselves. The Lord was up to something—that was plain enough for us to see—and we viewed ourselves more as willing participants in what He wanted for us than as people looking for the next thing to further our careers. I'm not saying we didn't put a lot of thought into what we did, but whenever we had a choice to make, we tried to make it prayerfully, waiting on the Lord.

He was the one with the music ministry, and He carried it out through us.

The Industry

Some years after the early days of Jesus music, there came a wave of bands and solo acts that seemed to be more concerned about being recognized and accepted as artists than about being effective musically or spiritually for the kingdom. These bands seemed to place their emphasis upon performance and appearance.

I think the main contributor to this mentality was the growth of the Christian music industry, both in popularity and in sales revenue. The idea that you could make a decent living and do positive music contributed to the proliferation of watered-down bands and largely ineffective presentations. This harks back to my earlier statement that just because you *can* do a thing doesn't necessarily mean you *should.*

When the record companies saw the potential for making lots of money, we started seeing ads and publicity geared to conformity. When I say conformity, I'm not talking about Christian bands becoming like one another; instead they seemed to become like whatever form of secular music was popular at the time. It wasn't long before the Christian music industry was advertising bands with slogans like, "If you like Van Halen, then you'll love so-and-so." The question in my mind was, *Why can't modern Christianity have a single original thought?* Christian music has come a long way since then, but at the time I was embarrassed to be associated with it.

Despite the progress made since the 1980s and early 1990s, I still see the latest secular trends reflected in Christian music. We had the copying of the boy bands, the girl bands, the rap bands, and the hip-hop bands. And now we're riding the wave of modern worship music, which also is flavored by secular music trends. I can often sing a popular secular tune right along with the new worship tune. The beat goes on.

At some points in history the world has copied Christian music. Man, how things have changed! Even with some of the more creative Christian bands performing today, I still hear the sounds of secular groups they're emulating. At the same time, ironically, Christian music remains distinct from its secular counterpart—in a bad way.

I can be in a new town, scan through the radio stations, and instantly tell when I've landed on a Christian radio station. The best way I can explain this is to say that the rock music doesn't have any real teeth, and the middle-of-the-road music sounds like it has been left out in the road too long. It's almost like it's trying to sound like the world only to a point; it stops just short of conveying something visceral.

The thing I like about some of the newer secular rock bands out there—bands like Mudvayne, Tool, Velvet Revolver, blink-182, Evanescence, Breaking Benjamin, and so on—is that the music has such great energy. I don't agree with much of the subject matter of their songs, but there's something about their sound that goes far beyond what some would call the devil's influence. You could take out all the vocals, and I would still enjoy their sound. Maybe it's the level of musicianship, the quality of the engineering, or an understanding of how to mix that type of music—or all of those—that makes it sound so good. But mostly, I think, it's the heart that comes through.

In Christian music, where's *our* heart?

It pains me to say that I've known plenty of non-Christian people who have had less of a destructive role through music than some "Christian artists." (I'm not going to name names.) There is seemingly no end to the contradictions you run into, whether they relate to an artist's intentions or to how his or her art comes about.

I know of one Christian artist, popular in the early 1970s, who had plenty of radio singles. My understanding was that most, if not all, her songs were written by a guy who wasn't even a Christian. I found that almost comical. Apparently it didn't matter whether the writer had a personal relationship with the Lord; the only thing that counted was throwing in the right hooks and Christian catch phrases.

But forget the songwriting, if you like; consider the artist. If he or she has the right look or has some other quality that is marketable, then that's all it takes to hit the road. It doesn't matter if the artist isn't well grounded in the faith or doesn't have much understanding of spiritual things. All that

"The Devil's Music"

On a recent night, while ministering at a church in Arizona, Deanne and I went for dinner at the house of one of the church's families. As the meal wound down, a conversation started that made me uncomfortable. With all his children present, the father asked me several questions about secular music.

I could tell this father was looking to me to affirm the way he had been discouraging his kids from listening to secular rock music. But I'm afraid I burst his bubble by not agreeing with much he had to say on the matter. I made it clear to him and his kids that while I believe it is better not to listen to certain groups based on the content of their songs, I do not think all secular music is "of the devil."

Based on the father's reaction, after a few minutes I realized I should keep my mouth shut or at least be more sensitive to what he was driving at. But oh no, I just kept plugging away with my views.

My intention was not to undermine this father in front of his seems to be important is that the artist can generate a lot of money for a record label.

I've known some artists who have gone out with the best of intentions, only to find themselves quickly in over their heads. Sometimes these artists are undone by their own popularity, unable to cope with their success. Many times they fall prey to temptations while on the road. Without spiritual depth and emotional anchors, they don't last long. These poor souls succumb to the fiery darts of the Enemy without even being aware they

kids. (And by the way, he never treated us with anything less than kindness.) But I just couldn't keep myself from commenting on some of the things he was putting out there. Finally, he looked at me and said, "Matt, now it's going to be harder than ever to get my kids not to listen to certain kinds of music."

I perhaps have a different take on music than do many Christians. I enjoy just about every form of music there is. (My least favorite, I suppose, would be bluegrass, but I still appreciate the level of musicianship it takes to play it well.) Friends are surprised when they realize that my collection of music consists of as many, if not more, classical CDs than any other style of music. Others are just as surprised to find out about some of the harder-hitting secular rock bands I listen to.

I do believe the saying "Garbage in, garbage out" is true, but just because a piece of music lacks mention of "Jesus," "God," or "Lord" every five seconds doesn't make it evil. I know there are a lot of sick, evil people doing music. It's just that I have a difficult time thinking of musical notes as having intrinsically evil properties.

have this very real Enemy who wants them to fail and, in the process, tarnish Jesus's name.

At their concerts, these artists have little of substance to say, and when they do speak, it's often a mere steppingstone to the next song. I know their efforts may be an attempt at doing a good thing. But it's unfortunate that in some cases these artists are put on the altar of inexperience to satisfy the greed of a company or individual, based on how they look or sound, without much thought about the spiritual ramifications.

Of Worship and Worship Music

In the last ten years, the business of worship music has become such a huge moneymaker that we've even had worship songs that address the issue of what worship has become for some of the writers! One song says, "I'm sorry, Lord, for the thing I've made it, when it's all about You." Though this is a good song, I have a difficult time singing it in church. To me, it sounds less like a congregational worship tune than a personal confession. I've never made worship anything other than what it is, so I have a hard time saying that I have.

I think the pitfall for worship-music writers is that many of them are on staff with some of the bigger record labels. I'm sure that at times these staff writers feel the pressure to crank out a "worship hit," and I don't know how they pull it off. I'm not saying that what they do is all wrong, but I know that for me, personally, it would be a monumental task to have to write a certain number of songs in a given amount of time or to write a song that deals with such-and-such assigned topic.

Most of the songs I've written over the years have come from a place of personal experience, but if I had to fill a certain quota of worship tunes, I might tend to write more from a position of what I thought people wanted to hear.

In almost every case, the songs that touch me the deepest, whether they are old hymns or newer songs, were written by someone who had suffered great loss or who had been through a spiritual or emotional trauma. I sense the heart of the writer when songs come from that perspective. But I sense this kind of authenticity all too rarely in the worship music of today.

Many of the songs we sing in church today are good songs, but there's something missing in them. They ring like a new composite quarter, not like the old quarters that were made of solid silver. The songs are often well crafted, lending themselves to full-band participation and choral arrangements. But in the end they lack real emotion and the ability to affect us any longer than it takes to sing the song. I know that not every song will affect everyone the same; it just seems to me that if we want to usher people into worship, it has to be done with more than bells and whistles.

This gets back to being called to do music ministry, not doing it just because we can. Our writing or performing of music for the Lord should be accompanied by His favor, His anointing, and not simply done through our own strength and natural talent.

Music, Narrowly

In 2002 Deanne and I went to Holland to participate in a conference looking at the arts from a Christian perspective. It was an interesting time for us, because we got to observe so many different art forms. For the most part, if you go to an artist-based event in the United States, it will focus mainly (if not exclusively) on music. But in Europe that's not the case. Here they had sculptors sculpting, photographers taking pictures, and ballet dancers dancing. They even had a guy who taught a class on how to make paper.

When I heard about that last one, I thought, *Why on earth would you want to make your own paper? Just go to the store and buy it.* But then a friend of mine from England, who was there teaching a class on photography, told me that he was going to take some of the paper-making classes when they didn't conflict with his own class schedule. He's a funny guy, so at first I thought he was pulling my leg. After a few days, though, he showed me some of the paper he had made. It was cool stuff. The paper became art in itself, some including bits of leaves or other materials. My photographer friend told me that after he got back home he was going to make different types of paper to print his photos on. I hadn't thought of that possibility, but it started making sense.

The conference organizers offered morning sessions, afternoon sessions, and concerts or other forms of entertainment in the evening. After the morning session, which usually consisted of worship and a message, the people leading classes would meet together in small groups to discuss the morning's message. Deanne and I were assigned to be leaders of one of these small groups. Every morning the same people were assigned to our table, so we got to know them fairly well.

One morning as we sat around our table, a guy from Australia by the name of John Smith and I got into a discussion about modern worship music. As the conversation progressed, John said to me, "As much as I love your country, with everything you've got going for you, I think you're really missing it when it comes to worship music."

At first I couldn't decide whether I should be offended or not, so I said, "Go on."

John continued by saying, "Look at the early Jesus-movement years.

The songs back then were largely written with the idea of 'we' instead of 'I.' They were much more focused on the collective community aspects of worship and not so focused on making it an individual endeavor."

I thought about some of the older worship songs, and I had to admit that maybe John was onto something. Back in the Jesus-movement period, we had a strong sense that we were in this Christian thing together, brothers and sisters. The Tuesday night Bible studies at Buck and Annie's house were a perfect example of how we worshiped and learned *together.* The songs of that time reflected the community quality of our faith. Was this something we were losing?

That night, when we gathered for the evening session, I decided I would take note of what types of worship songs we sang. Several groups from different parts of Europe led worship, singing their songs in their native tongues, with English translations projected on a screen. I quickly noticed that the vast majority of the songs European Christians had written were "we" and "us" songs. But the groups also threw in some songs from the United States—I guess to make us Americans feel more comfortable. Among these songs I was surprised to discover that the majority contained lyrics centered on "I" or "me."

For the rest of that evening, I tried to figure out what, if any, significance there might be in this new revelation. Maybe the prominent use of "I" in American worship songs is nothing more than an attempt on the songwriters' part to make people feel a personal connection with worship and with God. Still, I couldn't help reflecting on the many times that worship has exposed things I'm doing wrong, not just in my personal relationship with God but with other people. The Christian life in general and worship, particularly, is for the most part a group activity for the family of Christ. If worship is all about me and God, then I've got blinders on.

Hearts in the Right Place

My concerns with worship music go beyond the writers and musicians who make their living from the big record labels and reach right down into all the churches where modern worship music is sung. In particular, this concern is an issue for larger churches and the megachurches. Let me explain.

As churches grow and become centers for what some would call huge clubs, the tendency is for us to allow ourselves to view worship as a sort of spectator sport. We gather on Sunday morning and find ourselves caught up in a slick, professional kind of experience. We look on as the band and singers present a version of worship songs that is most enjoyable and acceptable. We appreciate the level of professionalism while allowing ourselves the liberty not to become involved personally in the worship experience. In essence, we go along for the ride.

I'm not just criticizing *others*. I have been guilty of the same thing myself. Over the years, I've found that as a worship band is doing its thing, one of two problems can occur for me: either the band is so good that I sit and listen without entering into worship (my producer brain takes over), or the band is so horrible that I'm distracted from worship. But I have found something that can cut through every issue of musical performance, and that is the attitude of the people who are leading worship.

For me, the best worship bands are the ones whose hearts are in the right place. This is an intangible thing, one that is difficult to explain. Yet it is something I have sensed in every kind of worship setting. I have heard bands that lacked the level of professionalism I've come to expect but, nevertheless, through their ministry, have found myself broken by the presence of God. I've also found myself at times equally broken while a band displays a wonderful level of musicianship. It doesn't seem to matter what style of music they play or how loud or soft it is; there just seems to be an intangible ingredient that makes whatever they do carry the weight of God's presence.

The times I've been able to speak with such bands after the service, I've found without exception that the singers seemed humble. Their performance was an extension of their own hearts. That is to say, they desired to get out of the way, to let God's glory come through. They became facilitators of worship, inviting God's presence to fill the sanctuary.

To me, it's a classic example of how God resists the proud but gives grace to the humble.

Despite my regrets about some of what's happening in Christian music today—and my openness to what's good in secular music—my own focus as a musician will always be toward the Lord. I don't know exactly what direction it will take in the future, as far as style goes, but I know my energies will be spent on doing some form of music that offers people a window into what being a Christian can mean. I know God has placed the gift of music in my life, not just for the sake of making good music, but also to glorify Him with my talents—to give back to Him in a tangible way the fruits of the gift He so freely gave me.

It's a hard thing to express, but for me, I sense God's pleasure when I sing to Him. And nothing pleases me more than when other people tell me that they also sense His pleasure when they listen to me sing.

18

Toward Eternity

My oldest brother, Irmen, died in January 2001—the first of the Ward siblings to move on. He was buried in the same Sacramento cemetery where my parents lie, and when I attended Irmen's funeral, that was the first time I had visited their grave since my father was buried.

Looking down at my parents' gravestones (each has a plaque listing all nine children, with me named there at the bottom) was a very emotional experience for me, as of course was Irmen's funeral.

That was the last occasion when Annie, Nellie, and I sang together. At the funeral service, we sang some of our old Second Chapter songs, such as "Consider the Lilies" and "Going Home," in our trademark three-part harmony. It was amazing how easily singing together came back to us.

Irmen had remained a Roman Catholic, and his funeral service was conducted by a priest. After the service, this priest (who had never heard of Second Chapter of Acts) came up to us and said, "That was really nice singing. I don't know if anyone's ever told you this, but you might consider going to a studio together and recording your songs. I think maybe you could go professional."

Even though we were at a funeral, with our oldest brother lying there in his coffin, we busted up laughing.

Where We Are Now

Annie and Buck are living amid the beautiful scenery of western Colorado. Annie still writes prolifically and performs occasionally, though not as much as she used to. Buck travels with her, runs her sound, manages her, and produces her music. I keep in touch with them regularly and go to visit them when I can. Once in a while, Annie and I will do a concert together. Nellie and Steve are living in Colorado as well. Since the end of Second Chapter, Nellie has been content not to sing in public. She has done a great job of raising her two children, Andrew and Jesse, now in their twenties. Steve, meanwhile, runs a video production company called Reel Productions. Our other siblings, except for Irmen, are still living—mostly in California.

My "perfect union" with Deanne holds strong. She works as a corporate leadership trainer and helps me with my career. What would I do without her? We still live in Colorado and travel frequently for my music engagements.

Meanwhile, our three daughters are growing up fast. As I write, Megin, our oldest, is twenty-one. She is married to Eric Pounds, who is currently serving in the Air Force. Our other two, Morgan (eighteen) and Mattie (sixteen), are still living at home, but not for many more years.

Time truly does fly by. But God is always good.

Faithful Forever

A number of years ago, the Lord taught me a lesson about His faithfulness:

Back when we were living in Lindale, Texas, I was sitting in our little country church one Sunday morning, while across the sanctuary sat the wife of a friend of mine. For some reason, I kept noticing her throughout the service and felt as though the Lord was trying to show me something about her. Then, as the service drew to a close, I had an overwhelming sense that I was to go and talk to her about something very sensitive. In my mind I was seeing a weird scenario played out: I was picturing myself confronting her about her having an affair.

Now, I had no evidence whatsoever that this woman was actually having an affair—no one had said a thing to me about it. And even if she was committing adultery, I had no idea who the other man in her life might be. Nor did I understand why I should be the one to speak with her about her sin. If I was wrong, wouldn't I embarrass her and make myself look foolish? So even though I had an overwhelming sense that I was supposed to speak with her, I told myself that I was suffering from an overactive imagination and talked myself out of addressing her.

A few weeks later this woman's husband came to me, distraught, and confided in me about an affair his wife was having with another man.

I asked him how long this had been going on.

He said, "A few weeks"—in other words, back to about the time when I had felt led to speak with her.

I was so blown away by this revelation that for a moment all I could do was to sit there with my mouth hanging open. When I regained my composure, I said to my friend, "I need you to forgive me for something."

He looked at me like I was nuts and asked, "Why on earth do I need to forgive you?"

I told him about how, a few weeks earlier, I had felt called to talk with his wife but had rationalized it away and in the end had said nothing to her.

"Oh, I see," he replied. "I really wish you would have spoken to her."

That was all he said, but I could tell he was upset with me. His obvious—and natural—hurt didn't make the pill of my disobedience any easier to swallow. You may be wondering what makes this a story of God's faithfulness. Well, I have learned from this experience, and from similar times in my life when I have fallen short of God's best, that my unfaithfulness to God doesn't make Him any less faithful to me. Although I was unfaithful by ignoring God's still, small voice about confronting the adulterous wife, He was faithful in speaking to me about her.

The faithfulness of God is something I can bank on. It doesn't change with the seasons. It doesn't depend on my goodness or gain strength from anything I can add to it. It stands alone as a testimony to the impartiality of God's character and sovereignty.

The Lord was faithful when He brought three insecure people together, through dire circumstances, gave them the name Second Chapter of Acts, and sent them out to help change the face of what was to become contemporary Christian music.

The Lord was faithful when He led me through the fires of cancer. And He was faithful yet again when He told me that I had more to do in His name after I was treated for the disease.

He has brought me through tornadoes, car crashes, earthquakes, and all manner of other "near misses" that could have taken my life at different times over the years. I can look back over my life so far and see His hand covering me, my family, my friends, and so many others. We are all safe so long as God has a purpose for us in this world.

I realize that someday I'll be laid to rest in the ground, just as my brother Irmen was. But in the meantime I still have some things here on earth that the Lord wants me to accomplish. The trick for me—for all of us—is to remain in that place where I'm willing to listen to God for guidance, to be obedient to what He asks of me, and to be prayerfully ready to carry out that mission.

Discography

Second Chapter of Acts

20 Years (1992)

Hymns Instrumental (1989)

Hymns 2 (1988)

Far Away Places (1987)

Hymns (1986)

Night Light (1985)

Together Live (1983)

Singer Sower (1983)

Encores (1981)

Rejoice (1981)

The Roar of Love (1980)

Mansion Builder (1978)

How the West Was One (1977)

To the Bride (1975)

In the Volume of the Book (1975)

With Footnotes (1974)

Matthew Ward

Even Now (2000)

My Redeemer (1997)

Point of View (1992)

The Matthew Ward Collection (1992)

Fortress (1990)

Fade to White (1988)

Armed and Dangerous (1987)

Toward Eternity (1979)

Acknowledgments

To Don Pape: without you this wouldn't have happened. Thanks for encouraging me to tell my story. Deanne and I will always be grateful for our friendship.

To Bruce Nygren, for all the editing help. Your talent and vision helped make the book what it is.

To Eric Stanford, for all the meetings at my house and Starbucks. Thanks for jumping in at the end. Your editing skills really helped the book be more focused and readable.

To the team at WaterBrook Press: Dudley Delffs, Leah McMahan, Ginia Hairston, Jeanette Thomason, Joel Kneedler, and Alice Crider. Thanks for all you've done to make the book a reality. Looks like there's a fun ride ahead.

To learn more about WaterBrook Press and view
our catalog of products, log on to our Web site:
www.waterbrookpress.com

WATERBROOK
PRESS

Printed in the United States
by Baker & Taylor Publisher Services